Table of Contents

Nova Walton-Marriott

ACKNOWLEDGMENTS

My (Grand) MOTHER-Janice Harris-Walton

Mommy. Thank you for loving me, sacrificing for me and taking me on to your already full plate with no hesitation. Thank you for teaching me about loyalty and family. Thank you for seeing greatness in me before I could see it. Thank you for supporting me from up above. I love you and miss you.

My Aunt-D.R.W

Thank you for all you've done to support my upbringing. Thank you for sacrificing your childhood to ensure I had one. I love you.

Daddy. Thank you for encouraging me to speak my truth so I could heal. Thank you for understanding the importance of letting me vent even when it was hard for you to hear. Thank you for finding the strength to go into recovery so I could see your talents re-emerge in my adult life. I love you.

Thank you to my Friend/Soror **Jodi** for writing the foreword and my Friend/Acupuncturist **Hyeon-Jin** for writing the afterword.

A special thanks to all the **Participants** in my survey and my **Beta Readers**. I appreciate your vulnerability and honesty.

Thank you to **Martha McAlpine** and **Lisa Fleet** for your contributions to my photo journal.

Thank you to my Sister/Friend **Vanessa** for helping me make this happen!

FOREWORD

As a child, my aunt who served as my "life teacher" would always give me sage advice. I can hear her repeat: "You will never have a testimony without a test", "Trust God always" and "Never lose your faith when the tough gets going". At the age of 16 I never understood the meaning behind these sayings but now, these words make perfect sense. My aunt was preparing me for the victories and the losses of life, to deal with adversity with integrity and to keep my head held high during every trial and tribulation. Most importantly, to understand that every decision or action I made had an equal repercussion or reaction (good or bad) and it was a direct result of my energy.

As an adult, I realize how determined my aunt was to provide me life's roadmap that I could not learn in a book or a classroom. She knew that life would be a cruel teacher but wanted to arm me with the emotional intelligence to make decisions that did not hurt or hinder me. That was her gift to me and it is a gift that has continued to serve as my compass to this day.

As I have witnessed through the various lives of my friends and loved ones, some Black women grew up without this compass and ultimately endured painful and hard lessons throughout life. However, most, if not all of my Black Queens persevered and usually triumphed over the immense pain and trauma introduced by family and their respective environments. Black women have had to shoulder generational curses and high expectations from family, friends and the universe. But we ALWAYS PERSEVERE. Nowadays, it's called #BlackGirlMagic but it has always existed within our ancestors and has been passed down generation after generation into our DNA.

In this memoir, Nova delves deep into her past to uncover her truth, her history and her memories to heal the wounds of her childhood and life. These words serve as her emancipation to freedom for her spirit and soul. As you turn the pages of this intense and honest memoir, one can only pray they would be as brave and resilient as Nova. Our journeys are written by God and Nova is on a path to discover peace and healing.

I wish my sister love and light. May her ancestors continue to protect her during her self-discovery and journey to healing.

Love, Jodi

PREFACE

My father inspired the title of this book. In the very first letter he wrote me from rehab, he said, "Baby girl, the sleeper has awakened". I believe his statement was representative of him finally coming out of the fog and becoming accountable for his actions. I found the title befitting to my own ascension out of the fog. He suggested I should consider writing a book because he felt I had something important to say.

I pondered on his suggestion and decided to give it a try. Who better to write about than myself? I know my story. I reasoned, I've lived a colorful life and besides, hanging my head in shame over past mistakes had become over-rated and sitting unhealed had become burdensome as well. I was tired of feeling judged and held hostage to the unspoken word.

This project is helping me walk in liberation despite the innuendo. It has opened the door for me to feel free to live, learn from my mistakes, heal and start fresh. For once, I don't care what other people think of me.

The theme derived from the deepest depression and frustration I've ever experienced. I've been harnessed by my past and held back as a result. I focused on my wants in lieu of what was best for me and deviated from my designated life journey. I don't want to block my blessings any longer because I know God has something great in store for the second half of my life. I want the freedom that comes with being totally lucid.

"You can't heal what you don't reveal"-Jay-Z

This book is a release. My "get past go card" to forgiving others and myself. I'm a grudge holder, especially when I can't make sense of something, but I realize what un-forgiveness is doing to me. It's hurting me more than anyone else because every time I revisit, I rip the scab off the wound.

I've spent the greater part of my life giving and trying to save others. I never felt worthy of being saved or maybe I just felt like being saved was unattainable. I've stayed in unhealthy relationships (intimate and familial) for longer than I should and under-estimated myself in life and career out of fear and low self-esteem. I've progressed in both areas but am not where I know I should be. My body image and maintenance has also suffered as a result of stress, poor eating habits and sleep deprivation.

I learned a tough lesson in how alone you can feel when you're going through something heavy and nobody really wants to hear it. They don't think I know but, people I held dear scattered like roaches because they didn't want to deal with my "aura" during some of the toughest times in my life.

After sacrificing so much, it's extremely important to me that my life be my own. I don't care to be "overly" obligated to anything or anyone at the moment. I want to do my part to the best of my ability and have it reciprocated, nothing more, nothing less.

My purpose is becoming clear. I want to build a legacy of my own instead of building someone else's. Besides my Son, my personal legacy begins with this book. It's the first thing I'm doing strictly for ME. Everything else I've done in life has been with someone else in mind. This project has brought healing I couldn't accomplish before, mainly because I'm being brutally honest with myself.

My affirmation for life is FREEDOM, mentally and financially. Both have made me more and more intrigued by entrepreneurship because I realize working for others restricts creativity. It requires you to conform and I've adjusted enough. I want the latitude to push the envelope, bring my thoughts to life, explore my options and travel to beautiful places. As I write my words down, I feel excited and rejuvenated. I can't recall ever feeling that way.

My past has created negativity, misery and bitterness to the point of altering my personality. My spirit was broken and when it began to hurt to smile, I knew I had to do something. I tried to avoid hurting others by retreating inward but have not been totally successful and I'm remorseful.

Once I got over the initial slump and felt strong enough to show my face, I started seeking ways to clean myself up internally. I discovered acupuncture, yoga/pilates and meditation. They have all become catalysts in my healing and self-awareness. I'm wounded but not a victim; I'm a good person.

I cried, prayed and wrote in my journal. Journaling created something tangible I can refer back to if I ever fall off track and also represents how far I've come. That undertaking led to this book. This book marks my progress and spans the beginning to the present.

I wrote my words in a decorative notebook and the note section of my cell phone and talked to a therapist, life coach and even my acupuncturist who has been an enormous source of support and more importantly, a FRIEND. Writing helped me become aware of how warped my thinking was and sometimes still is. In the beginning, my thoughts were so scattered I just scribbled aimlessly on the pages. The more I wrote, the more my words began to make sense. I was writing things I didn't even know I felt.

At first, I typed my thoughts into a word document. The life coach expressed to me the importance of writing my feelings down with a pen. I thought she was crazy at first because I didn't see the big deal in writing as opposed to typing. Believe me, there's a big difference. When you write, your energy flows differently. It's more time consuming than typing, you pause to think more and you're less apt to erase. It's rawer.

Throughout this book, I uniquely and intricately touch on trauma and how it affects your spirit, development and choices. I reveal traumatic events related to death/grief, abandonment, physical and emotional abuse, sexual violation, bullying, narcissism, heartbreak, teenage pregnancy, depression and domestic violence. I assure you, if you're not careful, trauma can be paid forward. Life is a huge cycle and before long, you're subconsciously passing your crap onto your kids and so on.

It has been very difficult to look myself in the eye. My intentions were good, I believed I knew what I was doing, but I had to admit I had been functioning according to EGO and a bit of narcissism (we all have those tendencies at some point in life) and needed God's help.

For a long time, God was the last one I was going to for help because I was angry and felt He was punishing me. All of a sudden, the baggage got too heavy. I was seeking relief in other people and constantly being let down and truthfully, I was absorbing too much negativity as well as projecting it.

I created, enhanced, and prolonged some of my terrible circumstances by failing to take responsibility. I got caught up in other people's offenses toward me and disregarded the part I played. It's not always the other person. Every time I got hurt, I didn't heed. I maintained the same routine expecting something different to happen next time. I thought, "One day, someone will appreciate the goodness in me and won't hurt me like all the others". I never looked at my own toxicity or unrealistic points of view.

Not negating the offenses but, had I been more cognizant of my baggage and tendencies, those people would not have been allowed to wreak havoc in my life. When the madness started, I would have disconnected a lot sooner. Some things were beyond my control, others could have been avoided.

"When you look at the world through rose colored glasses, red flags are harder to see".—
narcissist.sociopath.awareness

Nonetheless, I don't harbor many regrets because my choices got me HERE. They are a guarantee that one day I will be seasoned, whole within and able to set a good example because I'm finally doing the work to improve every day. I'm making strides to approach my present experiences from an optimistic point of view and reframe my past negative experiences because each one has a valuable lesson within.

I once read a book "The Alchemist" by Paulo Coelho; it changed my life. It helped me realize my past, although

9

messy, was all part of the bigger picture and in order to evolve I have to chalk it up to experience and count it all joy. I'm not saying I don't occasionally feel sorry for myself, wish things had gone MY way or even try to go against the grain occasionally. I do, but frankly, there's no future in sweating things I can't change or putting myself in a position to deal with undue stress.

Today, I choose to make my life count. I'm intelligent, spiritual, and insightful, but I don't know it all. My trials knocked me off my high horse and forced me to rely on God for every move I make. I'm totally engrossed in his desires for my life; invested in pleasing him. As a result, he's transforming me slowly but surely.

As parts of this work may be hard for some to read, I find it necessary to say this is about my healing, my clarity, my growth, MY TRUTH. While every piece of this work is the absolute truth, they are still my feelings and points of view. It's honest and detailed but not meant to be slanderous in any way. I pray the people involved will one day feel empowered to take a look at themselves as well and hope anyone caught in the crossfire of my pain will find it in their hearts to forgive me.

Message to my readers:

This memoir shares relatable experiences. The icing on the cake will be the influence it has on others. Perhaps

YOU the reader can identify similar patterns in your own life and be positively influenced to turn it around. I'm putting it all on the table and believe me, it hasn't been easy. There is always that little part of you that worries about being judged. I've also been challenged with being transparent and truthful while still trying to be tactful, humble and fair. I believe I found good balance.

I want you to know you're not alone. I want you to feel like you're sitting in each scenario as you read the book. My personal goal is to be a strong, positive blueprint because I still have my son, grand-daughter, siblings, nieces and nephews looking at me. Recovery and growth really can take place if you do the work. It all starts with YOU. God bless!

CHAPTER 1

Abandonment and Trauma

I was born in New York City to a 26 year old mother and a 17 year old father and raised by my paternal grandmother with my aunt's assistance. My biological mother, for her own personal reasons chose to walk away from her full-time parental obligation when I was an infant. I didn't know it at the time, but this decision would define my perception of self and open the door for many insecurities.

My grandmother was extremely loving and did all she could to ensure I was well taken care of. I was blessed to have her but I had voids. She provided a roof over my head, food in my mouth, a strong spiritual foundation, and a sound education that included a partial tenure in Catholic school.

Our family was tight-knit but not without fault. My grandfather was a functional alcoholic and would eventually move out of our home when he and my grandmother separated (they never divorced). Along with me, my grandmother raised five children (four sons and one daughter). I had a conventional childhood in a quiet

12

Queens suburban neighborhood. We lived in a single-family home where I shared a bedroom with my aunt.

Although my mother had chosen to move on, she did visit occasionally and my grandmother never turned her away. These visits were very uneasy for me as I was not bonded with her and did not trust her. Her presence made me extremely anxious because I knew her visits would involve a request to take me to her home for an extended stay. There were also times she would ask me to just go out with her for the day and promise to bring me home afterward. I agreed a few times but she always broke the promise and I would be stuck spending the night. I resented that.

Generally, no matter how much I resisted, fought or begged, my grandmother would honor her request and force me to go home with a person I barely knew and did not feel comfortable with. She would visit, take me for a few days, buy me a few things, show me off to her friends, bring me back and return to her life. Her visits were scattered over months, sometimes years and of her own convenience as no formal agreement was put in place. It was like getting dumped over and over again and I really had no choice in the matter.

I recall an occasion she came to visit, asked to take me home with her and I fought adamantly. My grandmother and aunt told me we were going to take a ride to see her house and come back home. We took the cab ride to the city, arrived at her home, and sat for a bit.

A while later, my grandmother and aunt told me they were going to the store and would be right back. I asked to go but they assured me they were returning. They never did. The worst thing you can do is lie to a child. I remember crying profusely because I was left behind. To this day, being left behind is a serious trigger for me.

Another time, she came to pick me up in the middle of the night from my brother's mother's house without my knowledge. She was taking me to Baltimore for her mother's funeral. While sleeping, I felt someone pick me up and carry me out of the house. When I looked up, I was in a car. My communion dress was hanging there and I didn't even know where I was going. I felt like I was being kidnapped. We went to her friend's house in the city and spent the night, went out the next day to buy new clothing and later that night, another good friend of hers drove us to Baltimore. This trip exposed me to family members I didn't even know I had to include two siblings I had never met (an older brother and sister). I was seven years old at the time.

I felt like everything with my mother was forced, a forced "mother-daughter relationship", forced to call her "mommy", forced to go home with her etc. She made it extremely difficult to bond with her because she believed she deserved the respect of a mother, but never really put the work in. She didn't realize the gap in relationship and the healing that needed to take place. She didn't understand she needed to approach the situation gently and first form a bond, that buying me presents and exposing me to famous people was nice but wasn't going to make me more endeared to her. I didn't care about notoriety. Her presence wasn't non-existent, it was sporadic and she would try her best to fulfill material requests when I had them.

One year, in between homes and staying with relatives, I ran downstairs on Christmas morning and there was not one present under the tree for me. I thought I did something wrong that "Santa" skipped over me; I was nine years old. My grandmother comforted me and told me he was just running late. Later that afternoon, my Godfather showed up with a bunch of stuff. That evening, my grandmother took me to my mother's house in Brooklyn where there was a tree and gifts waiting for me. She gifted me a "Coleco-Vision" game system, a Care Bear and a few other gifts. But, holidays with her were inconsistent as well.

One day on a rare occasion I agreed to go out with her, we were sitting in a restaurant and she tried to tell me my father wasn't my real father. She tried to convince me that the Caucasian man at the restaurant with us was my "real" father. I was so devastated I excused myself from the table and immediately ran to a payphone (my grandmother always made sure I had a quarter in my pocket to call home if I needed to).

I called my aunt hysterically crying and she and my father came to pick me up that evening. My aunt comforted me and told me it wasn't true. My father commenced to abrasively ask me, "Who's your fucking father?!" I was so shook up I didn't respond; I just sat in the car and cried. I was 10 years old.

My mother never took responsibility for her mistakes. I attempted to address the elephant in the room a few years ago and instead of atoning, she pointed the finger at others, insinuating that my grandmother and family "took me away from her and poisoned me against her". My grandmother never spoke an ill word against her to me and never impeded her contact with me. My impression of her was all my own. I felt abandoned by her and like she could never find it in herself to be **fully** active in my life. There is so much more to mothering than gifts and a good time.

"One of the most important relationships we have is the relationship we have with our mothers".—Iyanla Vanzant

During my upbringing, I was blessed to have a few people step into motherly roles in my life, to include my brother's mother. Unfortunately these relationships also tended to be of convenience. That's the thing about playing a

16

motherly "role", the person is not obligated to stay. A "*mother*" is supposed to be there consistently, no matter how much they have to juggle. A mother loves unconditionally. My grandmother and grandfather provided the only unconditional love I have ever had in my life. They didn't have to stay, they chose to.

My grandmother never made a difference between me and her biological children, she just added me to the fold. It definitely caused some tension with her two youngest children though. She was the most selfless person I have ever known. Still to this day I've never met anyone like her. She was a mother in every sense of the word.

All I saw from her was great sacrifice. I watched her wash clothes by hand in the tub with a scrub board because we didn't have a washing machine and iron clothes with a manual iron that had to be heated on a gas burner when our electricity was cut off. I've also seen her hold a small pot of food over burning candles to heat it when our gas was cut off.

As an adult, I recall her coming home from work hungry and scarfing down a pack of ramen noodles cooked in cream of chicken soup with sliced onions on top because she didn't have the money to buy breakfast or lunch for the day. She never complained; just rose to the occasion. She was the epitome of woman and my love and loyalty always has and always will lie with her and my aunt for

17

stepping up the way they did.

Lord knows where I would have been without my grandmother; she saved my life. She never showed her pain on her face and never tossed me to the wind, not even in times of adversity. She did her best with what she had and what she knew, and instilled the importance of family in me, almost to a fault. I can survive in very adverse situations by experience and witnessing her perseverance.

All of that said, I still wonder how my self-perception could have been shaped differently had my parents upheld their responsibility when they decided to have me. One thing I will say about my grandmother is she didn't like me to speak badly about my father and never allowed me to speak badly about my mother either. Her favorite line was, "You mustn't hate". She knew my father's shortcomings but favored him, and if I spoke a word against him she would lash out at me.

She stressed to me that I should never turn my back on him no matter what; she even made me promise her on her death bed. She used to say, "your father has special love for you, he's just sick". On two isolated occasions, angry at me because I spoke ill of him out of anger and disappointment, she told me if I hated her son she hated me too. She also insinuated that my mother raped her son because of their age difference. I knew she was just angry but that statement made me feel even more useless and unwanted. I used to tell myself, "Why didn't they just abort me? I'm suffering from their irresponsibility!"

My father lived in the home and was allowed to be active in decision-making and discipline (at times, he could be a bit too authoritarian). He provided a source of income for a few years but my grandmother and aunt were the primary caretakers and nurturers in my life. As a baby, I was a daddy's girl. My grandmother often told me stories of how I would shake my crib and scream out "Dada!" when he entered the house and how he couldn't leave without first putting me to sleep.

My fondest memories of my father involve him taking my brother and me to what we deemed the "fish park" on Merrick Boulevard or "80 park" in Jamaica, Queens. There we would play on the swings and monkey bars and watch my dad rock people on the basketball court. He was handsome, extremely athletic, and musically inclined as he could sing and play the piano by ear. He earned a living as a singer and musician for a number of years as well as participating in some illegal activity. My mother was and still is an entertainer by profession.

When my dad turned to drugs, I lost him. I no longer had that love, kindness, affection, guidance or positive blueprint. He turned into someone very ugly; someone else that abandoned me. He chose drugs and women

19

over me and it set the stage for serious daddy issues causing me to seek that love and validation in men. There were times my father made me feel more like his parent or provider than his child.

He would say things like, "I don't need to make my own plate, that's what I have a daughter for". Years later, when he lived with me I would ask him to seek employment and help with food. I was working multiple jobs, taking care of my household on my own and after paying all bills, sometimes came up short. His response was, "How do you work two jobs, and you don't have any money?"

As a child and growing teenager, he made it difficult to discuss concerns with him because of his "macho" approach. I was afraid to tell him when I got my period because I knew it would result in him imposing more unnecessary rules upon me. I was afraid of him and resented him. There were times the mere sound of his voice scared the shit out of me. I looked at him as "The Enforcer".

I recall being punished and confined to my room for the day for accidentally wetting the bed. As a parent, I didn't punish my son for things like that, I just ensured he went to the bathroom before bed and occasionally woke him up to use the bathroom in the middle of the night to avoid it happening. My father was hard on me.

"When I'm at my best, I am my father's daughter."–

Unknown

As loving and attentive as my grandmother was, it didn't replace the crucial components that only a mother and father can provide. Their absence set the stage for insecurities in adulthood because although I was aging, parts of me remained stuck as that wounded little girl. I was insecure and never felt protected. Although I have lots of happy memories from my childhood, I also recall feeling cheated and wondering where I fit in.

I have always been sensitive and felt very deeply which makes it easy for me to take on the emotions of others. I don't want anyone to be hurt because I know how it feels. I over-extend, I'm loyal and very protective of who I love. I would do anything for anyone. On the other hand I can also be very rigid, defensive, untrusting and have a terrible temper. I've been in fight or flight mode for the greater part of my life.

I used to look at all my friends with parents in the home and think, "Why didn't mine care to be there on a full-time basis? Why were they so selfish?" I latched on to any decent woman (father or uncle's girlfriends, family friends or otherwise) that paid me any mind because I enjoyed the love and affection I received from them, I craved it. I felt like I always had to "people please" or cling in order to feel special.

My grandmother did her best but she was being pulled in

21

many directions. She sang to me on my birthday and as a gentler way of waking me up in the morning (Good morning to you, Good morning to you, we're all in our places with sunshiny faces; and this is the way to start a new day). She always made me feel like no one could ever replace me in her heart and literally made sure I knew she loved me like she'd given birth to me herself but, she wasn't MY mother that I could call my own. She never did anything to make me feel this way but I always felt in constant competition for a place in her life. She catered to all of our insecurities so we all felt special in her heart, she spread herself thin.

My brother's mother once said to me, "I always wondered why Mommy loved you so much, what's so special about you?" Again, she played a motherly role in my life and bought me things but the minute she thought I was getting more attention than my brother, the gloves would come off and the role would shift.

I also felt like I was playing a game of tug of war with my aunt who seized every opportunity to remind people she was the daughter and I was the grand-daughter. It made me feel minimized and motherless all over again. She maintains it was innocent but that doesn't take the pain away.

My aunt played a motherly role too and was my primary caretaker. She sacrificed a lot but I know it wasn't completely voluntary; it was dumped on her. She was only 13 when I was born, I assume she really didn't want the responsibility of taking care of someone else's child. I love her for it though, no matter the reason, and I know she loves me. I just want her to know I was never trying to take her mother away, I just wanted the security of having one consistently.

When I was a child, she got up in the morning to get me ready for school and do my hair, did homework with me, helped me study for tests, went on school trips, took me on her dates, and clothed me when she had the funds. We were very tight and I looked up to her but as I matured, I could feel her resentment toward me and the responsibility. She often projected her own unhappiness onto me by saying and doing hurtful things. She would lash out in anger, forget her words once calm and expect things to go back to normal between us the next day. When I held a grudge, I was deemed the unreasonable one. I showed my love for her through materialistic gestures, affection and my words as well but I don't think she ever realized how much I loved and appreciated her for all she had done and how her negative actions tore me apart inside.

Because my grandmother had to work every day, my aunt was her go-to person for my care, even if my father was present in the home and could have done it himself. When he turned to drugs, he stopped being involved in parenting me until it was time to discipline me. He wasn't often held accountable to his responsibilities.

To provide balance in my narrative, I have many pleasant childhood memories to include weekly visits from both sets of great-grandparents and big family dinners. It wasn't unheard of for my grandfather or father to randomly play the piano and sometimes, my aunt and uncles would sing along. On Thanksgiving, my grandmother always made a big spread of food and desserts with my aunt's assistance and invited everyone over.

EVERY YEAR, my aunt took us to church on Easter and made a huge wicker basket with every candy you could think of; each one of us had our own chocolate bunny. She, my grandmother, my brother's mother or my godfather always made sure I had a nice outfit and my aunt ensured my hair was neatly groomed. On Halloween, she dressed us up, decorated the house, took us trick or treating and checked candy for harmful objects; she even carved a pumpkin once in a while.

On Christmas, she always hand-picked a real tree (it always had to be real and the right size) and decorated it beautifully and in later years, she threw annual New Year's Eve parties and brought the family together for beach outings on the 4th of July. She was really into the holidays and really into family.

She also threw huge backyard parties with her and her

band providing the entertainment. She's an awesome singer by profession and would occasionally allow me to attend her gigs at a Brooklyn nightclub when I was a teenager. I was her biggest fan and would sit front and center to watch her sing.

I had two older cousins that took me under their wings, spent time with me and showered love on me constantly. One would take me for weekend sleepovers and the other would sit and watch "Little House on the Prairie" with me when we lived in their house for that year. I visited my great-aunt and uncle in upstate New York on school breaks and during the summer and really enjoyed going to work with my grandmother.

Annual church trips to "Bear Mountain" and "Rye Playland" with my great-grandmother and cousin also have a special place in my heart. She would pack a cooler full of food and keep us out there the whole day. We'd get back late and she would wake us up bright and early to go to mass on Sunday.

At least once every other month, I'd meet my grandfather at work, we'd pick my great-grandfather up and go to "Galaxy Diner" in Brooklyn for dinner; we always had the best time. My other aunt picked me up on weekends whenever I asked, allowed me time with her and my little cousins and gave me a minute to be a kid. And, I had a Godfather who stepped up to the plate, gave me his time and treated me well. I've always held on to those memories because they're the best I've ever had. As we started losing integral family members, the dynamic began to change.

After the age of nine, my home life became tumultuous as addiction began to rear its ugly head amongst my grandmother's sons. It started before that but, that's when it became really bad. For as long as I can remember, physical fights often took place between the siblings (to be expected). But, I was approximately five years old (maybe younger) when I witnessed my first but not last domestic dispute between my father and one of his significant others. I was often awakened by loud banging noises from our dining room and would run to the top of the staircase to sit there and listen.

I saw the elder male figures in my family treat their wives fairly well but I never saw that in my immediate circumference. The men in my household were abusive toward women with exception to two of my uncles; I've never seen either one of them hit a woman.

I saw my father beat one of his girlfriends because she stood up to him in front of his friend. She addressed him because he sent me upstairs to her with a joint in my hand. I was about six years old at the time and that taught me I should never assert myself with my man or I would get my ass kicked.

I also witnessed my grandfather come home drunk on many occasions and start arguments with my uncles, aunt or grandmother. He was always very good to me and I never landed in his line of fire, but his actions left an impression. Honestly, I believe he was the catalyst for all the addiction in our home.

Still, we had a very close relationship and would often eat breakfast together (slab bacon, over-easy eggs, grits and toast-made by him) or sit in front of the television spending time and eating "Mr. Salty" pretzels with milk (for me) and beer (for him).

Nevertheless, his presence often changed the energy in the household negatively and eventually he moved out. I went from seeing him every day to occasionally. We were best buddies despite his behavior and now he was gone too.

At the age of seven, I was touched inappropriately by a family member. Fast asleep in my pink pajamas, I felt someone pull the back of my pants down. He didn't penetrate me, he rubbed his penis in between my cheeks until he ejaculated. I laid there awake, back toward him and stiff as a board until he finished. When he was done, I quickly slid out of the bed, went to the bathroom, cleaned myself up, and ran down the hall to my grandmother's room to get in bed with her where I felt safe. I never said a word while it was happening and I don't know exactly who it was because I never looked at him and didn't look back when I left the room. I never told my grandmother.

Thankfully, it never happened again however it was enough to ignite a form of promiscuity in me; it took my innocence away. I started doing unorthodox things for a young child, wanting to kiss little boys, playing "house", calling people my "boyfriend", getting felt up on the side of my house by one of the neighborhood boys, etc. I basically moved faster than a young child should.

One day while visiting a neighbor I was playing "house" with one of her sons and attempting to do what parents do (naturally, we didn't know what we were doing). Our pants were down and we were pretty much humping each other. His sister walked in the room and caught us. She didn't tell my grandmother or her mother but she did tell all the kids on the block. That was worse.

I was teased for years over that and known as the little girl who did nasty things with the neighbor (if only they knew where the behavior came from). I was humiliated daily and didn't even know I was wrong.

My social life wasn't much better as I struggled to fit in amongst my peers. I had a best friend I loved dearly but, the neighborhood kids would pit us against each other by telling her I called her a name or had negatively addressed her skin color. Through it all, this was my only friend and remains a dear friend; more like a sister.

I have struggled with socialization my whole life because I could never fully trust and had unrealistic expectations of what friendship was supposed to be. I tried too hard and wanted to be liked. I looked up to all the wrong people and sometimes tried to emulate them because I thought they were cool and had the confidence I wanted. Honestly, they probably could have learned more from me than I ever could from them.

I had great things to offer the world too, I just didn't use my voice back then. Their ability to assert themselves and walk with confidence caused me to hold them in high esteem and believe they had an advantage over me. I wished I had the courage to conduct myself that way. My overt negative sense of self liberated them to push me into the shadows and make me feel less than. I allowed it.

In school, I experienced rejection from my peers and shied away from socializing with them so I wouldn't continue to get hurt. In turn, I would often organize games with first and second graders and spend my recess with them. I was safer that way.

We lived in my stable childhood home until I was eight years old before we had to move. My grandmother lost her house over my grandfather's irresponsibility. She went from owning her home to renting and life changed immensely. Until we could find a new home, we were forced to split our family up. I was transferred from

Catholic to public school of my own volition. My grandmother gave me a choice but, had I told her I didn't want to transfer, she would have killed herself to keep me in private school even with us being homeless.

I stayed with my brother's mother for a little while because my new school was on her side of town but that was short-lived. I think I had an accident in my brother's car bed or maybe she just didn't want the extra responsibility; she was also struggling with drugs. I have always loved her and know she loves me in her way, but her love is conditional. I'm good with her as long as I'm doing things her way. I could never do enough to prove to her that she was amongst the top of my list.

My best memories with her are laying on her lap while she cleaned the wax out of my ears with a bobby pin (that always felt so good) or laying on the bed with her and my brother playing a game called "bull-mess" and watching my brother imitate "Ralph Kramden" from an episode of "The Honeymooners". Those were always fun times filled with laughter. I also appreciated the love she has always so freely given my Son. That's his Grandma.

Christmas was also a huge deal for her, she would stack gifts up on the walls for my brother and me and loved to see the smiles on our faces when we opened them but, would talk about it for years. That made me feel resentment because it removed my free will to process her gestures and exhibit appreciation.

I did appreciate all she did but she has always made me feel indebted to her for her contribution to my life and has occasionally embellished how large that contribution was. The pressure cheapened the experience. She referred to me as her "daughter" only when certain people were around. At my brother's repast, she referred to me as his older sister and it crushed me. Still, I know she too comes from a past of hurt and abandonment so I don't hold anything against her. I just choose to stay away to preserve my peace. I love her and wish her well. She did the best with what she had.

After staying with her for a bit I went to live with my grandmother at her brother's house. She and I shared a room with a single bed. I was a wild sleeper so, instead of putting me on the floor, she put me in the bed and slept on the floor. We stayed there for my entire fourth grade year.

My first year in public school was horrible. I spent the first half of the year in one school and the second half in another. In the first school, I was bullied by a group of girls. I was overzealous and tried to fit in and they didn't like me.

Twice after school they jumped on me, once in the park and once on the handball court. It was so traumatic I still remember their names. No one helped me either time, not even the friends I was walking home with. I got up off the ground, dusted myself off and went home. The next day I got up and went to school, sore and scared like nothing ever happened. I never told the teacher or my grandmother because she had enough to worry about. The bullying continued into my fifth grade year until I began to fight back. I've been fighting back ever since, in and outside my household.

My grandmother was told about a vacant home by a family friend and we moved in at the end of the school year, but life was never the same. The new house was a lot smaller than the old one. We named it "Little House on the Prairie" after my favorite television show. We were all on top of each other and the drug addiction in my house became a lot worse.

My uncles and father were stealing from my grandmother, aunt, and me and by the time I was 12 years old, my father had become physically abusive. My anger and resentment caused me to lash out. I stood up for what I thought was right and he didn't like that.

If I had a few dollars in my pocket I would have to spend it quickly because if he found out, he would take it. I recall him busting my lip and choking me so hard his nail marks were in my neck over five dollars. One of my uncles stood there and watched. My grandmother knew I had the money and told me not to tell him about it if he asked.

When I told her what he had done and that he took it by force, she told me I should have just given it to him. Imagine my disdain being inadvertently told it was my fault I was assaulted over MY money.

It was not unheard of for the neighborhood drug dealer to show up at our door to collect a debt and my grandmother or aunt would just pay it. Over the years, our house has been raided by police a few times. I have had my bedroom destroyed in a search, my door taken off the hinges and have even witnessed my grandmother in handcuffs because of her son's indiscretions. She was an enabler more than my aunt but she didn't deserve any of what she was put through. Everything she did was out of good intention and love for family.

I also believe she overcompensated with her kids because although she shared a tight bond with her father, she didn't have a great relationship with her mother. I witnessed my great-grandmother treat her unkindly on numerous occasions and it hurt her feelings deeply, sometimes to the point of tears. She felt my great-grandmother favored her sons and through my observation, she went on to favor her sons once she became a mother.

I'd watch them walk out of the house to sell her belongings and she would do nothing about it. I'd call her at work to tell her what was happening and she would say,

"Don't say anything, just let them go". She did a lot of yelling but there were never any real consequences for their actions. She would just say, "They're sick".

To add insult to injury, my father continued to have children and she would render support every time. Out of seven kids, my grandmother and aunt raised five full time and one brother intermittently.

I learned how to be co-dependent, an enabler, and tolerate much too much from a man by watching my grandmother and aunt. My grandmother never let anyone fall and I adopted those same qualities. She stayed married to my grandfather through infidelities, extra-marital offspring, alcoholism, and emotional abuse.

Even after separation, she allowed him into the home and cooked him a birthday dinner of his favorite neck bones and kidney beans with rice every year. There were even times he didn't show up. I've seen evidence of his infidelity and was even introduced to one of his mistresses. When I voiced anger or disappointment, she would tell me her issues with him had nothing to do with my relationship with him; that I needed to operate based on how he treated me not how he treated her. She got her heart broken over and over again by her spouse and children and never turned her back.

I watched my aunt enter numerous long-term relationships, be emotionally abused, cheated on and used for the greater part of my life and hers. I saw her taken advantage of by our own family as she has for many years been the financial go-to person. She too, never turned her back.

I grew up believing it was okay for the woman to "hold it down". The men in my life were never held to any type of standard. I revered my grandmother and aunt and never wanted to believe any example they set was wrong. I eventually went on to support men many times without ever having it reciprocated.

My father and uncles were hustlers for the most part and honestly, my grandmother was too; just in a positive way. My grandparents were the only people in my household to hold nine to five jobs consistently. My grandmother worked for the City of New York and my grandfather was a hospital police officer, both retired from those roles.

I definitely get my strong drive, work ethic and troubleshooting skills from my grandmother. I spent short spurts of time unemployed but I'm a very hard worker and have consistently maintained employment for over 25 years. I'm book smart but also street smart by watching my surroundings and functioning in my upbringing.

I also developed a habit of maintaining secondary employment as a safety net because I refused to be in a position to go through any of the hardship I experienced with my family. My son has never lived under any of those conditions by the grace of God. There are times we struggled but I made a way.

Growing up I felt trapped and miserable in my household. I felt like a built-in babysitter because my father kept having kids but refused to care for them. I resented him because he took part of my childhood away. I couldn't go anywhere without one of my siblings in tow and couldn't receive a gift without him insisting that my siblings should receive one too. With addicted parents, it's common to end up taking on their responsibilities because they don't want to be bothered.

His drug habit was out of control and every time I got something nice (a bike, a TV, a piano) he would steal and sell it. My first memory of intermittently being without utilities took place in this house. I used to think, there are grown human beings living here and nobody can help keep the damn lights, water or gas on? My aunt was the only one contributing when she could and my father contributed sporadically when he was still singing part-time to make a living.

Money was always tight but my grandmother always made a way. A talented seamstress, she made vests for a local motorcycle club, dresses for an occasional wedding and did alterations for a neighbor who owned a dry cleaning business to make extra money. She always made sure I was clothed even if she had to make them herself. I've had plenty of graduation and Easter dresses made by her. We all have.

She made meals that stretched such as fricassee chicken, a big pot of spaghetti with tomato paste and frankfurters and an occasional treat of homemade peanut butter cookies. Once in a while, she was able to bulk shop at "Gouz" supermarket and we had food and good juice to drink for a week or two. We didn't have a lot but she would still offer an outsider a plate of food and take someone in to live if they didn't have a place to go. We often joke, our family is known to take in strays.

I would gain reprieve from that environment when she allowed me to go to work with her. On those days I could be a kid. I always wanted to be a teacher and loved to play school so she would put me in her office conference room with a chalk board, give me a bunch of paper, pens, pencils, and folders and go back to her desk. I was always content being by myself.

I sat there quietly all day teaching my imaginary class until she came to take me for lunch at McDonalds or allowed me to go across the street to Kennedy Fried Chicken to buy coffee iced cream. She usually took me to work with her on a Friday (pay day) and we would visit my great-grand parents in the Bedford-Stuyvesant area of Brooklyn after we left the job. We would spend a little time with family and my great-grandmother, a devout catholic cooked fish on Friday so we would eat dinner before heading home for the weekend. Those were perfect days, but we always had to return home.

My grandmother also believed in moving forward, mostly without resolution. Out of frustration, I often tried to voice my feelings about the things that were happening but she instructed me not to discuss it in or outside the home. I guess that's how she coped. As I grew, I learned to bury my feelings and block things out, to act like I didn't care about the shit going on around me. Suppressing all of that made me angry and bitter and I began to rebel by the time I became a teenager.

I returned to private school in the sixth grade and kept my zeal for learning but that changed when I entered the seventh grade. My grades began to drop and besides a few notable accolades such as Student of the Month and 1st place in the school spelling bee, I graduated with subpar grades.

That fall, I entered a high school two train rides and one bus away from home and for at least eight to ten hours a day I WAS FREE! When I got a taste of that freedom I took full advantage. I got with the wrong group of girls and began to cut classes. It was exhilarating until it caught up to me. I was failing all my classes and my aunt was grounding me for whole marking periods but I didn't care. Her favorite go-to punishment was "You got a day in the house". No one ever asked me what was troubling me, they just did a lot of yelling and grounding. I used school time to have freedom. Even if I walked the streets or sat on a park bench, I had peace for a few hours.

At age 13 I began dating my first boyfriend who was four years older and a neighborhood drug dealer. I was fascinated with guys in the street, guys that reminded me of what I saw in my house. He was a nice guy and respectful to my family as far as I could tell but as I look back, I'm not completely sure if he didn't plant himself in my house as a potential provider of drugs to my father and uncles.

I met him while walking from the store one day. I was always very shapely for my age and he chased me up the hill and asked if he could talk to me for a minute. He was short, brown-skinned with almond shaped eyes and a curly top haircut. We stood there and talked for a few and before long, he was coming up the hill to my house daily to visit. I liked him and enjoyed his company but we dealt with each other for about 5 or 6 months before he moved on.

Living in that environment, the only bit of solace I had was when I was able to go across the street to a friend's house for the day or to spend the night. It gave me the opportunity to be in what I thought was a traditional family setting with a mother and father. They always had food on the table and nice clothes to wear, went to church on Sunday, and made me part of the family. I spent as much time in that house as I could or around the corner at another good friend's house.

In my ninth and tenth grade years, I began to voluntarily have contact with my mother and she gave me keys to her house. By that time, she was living in Queens and gave me free reign to come there whenever I wanted. The contact served two purposes- I was making an effort to get to know her and I needed another form of escape from my situation at home.

I was in high school, the peer pressure was on and the demand increased to fit in and wear cool clothes. Back then, everyone was wearing the colored 54.11 classic Reeboks and Champion sweatshirts. I don't recall ever having a Champion sweatshirt back then but I did have the reeboks, only black or white though, because they matched everything. I was still able to skate by amongst my peers.

She would sometimes buy me things my grandmother couldn't afford to and my grandfather would buy me a pair of sneakers here or there. I occasionally spent the night at her house, most often, taking a friend with me or she would meet me at school and spend a few hours with me.

Things went well for a bit but she always became

overbearing after a while. When displeased with me she would aggressively pull the "I'm your mother" card. It was like she always had to announce who she was. It completely turned me off and I'd distance myself again. I would think, "Why can't she just chill?" She had a tendency to talk condescendingly and I resented that. I was willing to try to build a friendship but a mother/daughter relationship was off the table regardless of who she was by birth.

She was serving a purpose in my life, provided an escape out of a tumultuous situation, and helped me fit in at school a little more. I didn't feel any remorse about asking her for things, I felt she owed me. I realize now how wrong I was as she was just doing all she could to extend an olive branch. She could have done better in some areas but I was wrong for being disrespectful and using her for my own agenda.

I didn't know her story, I didn't really know her. I never asked about her life, I just formed conclusions by what I saw with the naked eye. She presented herself in a manner that alluded to her having her shit together. From my vantage point, she had nice things but bounced around a lot and never seemed stable. Collectively, I didn't respect her for neglecting her responsibilities, for failing to choose ME first.

Ultimately, I finished the school year failing miserably and had to attend summer school in order to progress to the next grade. When I was 15, my family moved again...

CHAPTER 2

Spiraling Out of Control

We moved into a new house in the summer, a larger home, but the conditions remained the same. Still looking for ways to escape, a friend of mine told me about a boarding school in Mississippi she would be attending in the fall and I jumped at the opportunity. This would be the perfect way to get out of my house! Once again, I went to my mother for help because she always seemed to make big things like that happen.

A good friend of hers helped her buy all I needed to attend and another friend of hers drove us down to the school. The school sat on grounds reminiscent of a college campus and my living quarters were in a dorm setting with a residential coordinator on duty. This arrangement was a great opportunity for me as it prepared me for life on my own and gave me academic focus.

My grades began to improve and I quickly became an A/B student. I played snare drum in the band and sang in a chorus that I travelled with occasionally. I also met people from all over the world. However, the need to fit in remained with me and any form of rejection from my peers left me hurt and disappointed. It bent me out of shape that I didn't fit in and before long, I was feeling like I wanted to go home. I had the break I needed.

I escaped dysfunction, but I also missed it and my grandmother. I didn't see the gift in the opportunity to live independently. My old life was familiar and comfortable like a broken-in shoe. My grandmother accepted my daily collect calls and allowed me to come home for Thanksgiving and Christmas breaks but that wasn't enough. The visits only strengthened my desire to return home. Not unlike drug addiction, family dysfunction is an addiction as well. Without careful and intentional forward movement, both mentally and physically, positivity will seem wrong, the dysfunction will feel right.

To add insult to injury, when I returned to school from Christmas break, I was entering the cafeteria for breakfast and was called over by the principal, seated at a table with a few other school officials. He asked if I had spoken to my mother as she had not yet paid my school bill. Shocked and embarrassed, I just said NO and walked away. She made a way for me to be admitted to the school but wasn't able to sustain it. My grandmother was left holding the bag. I never communicated my conversation with the principal to my mother or grandmother, I used that encounter as a mental excuse to ask my grandmother to come home for good. I told her I was homesick and did not want to be there anymore. She let me stay after I came home for spring break and enrolled me at a local public high school.

Almost immediately, I fell back into bad habits and began to skip school again. My grades quickly declined. My home situation wasn't any better as the addiction was still in place and my father was physically abusive as ever. I stayed out of the house as often as I could and continued to rebel. I even cut off all my hair and pierced my nose. My tenth grade year ended with another stint in summer school but I didn't mind because it gave me a reason to get out of my house.

I entered 11th grade with the same mindset. I left home in the morning, went to homeroom and exited the school through the back door. I liken my predicament at that time to drug addiction. When you're high, you don't think about your problems. When you're down, the problems come flooding back. Most of my time at boarding school was a high. When I returned home, the problems immediately came flooding back and my attitude shifted to accommodate the situation. I was no longer motivated to do well.

Troubled, feeling a little regret, hurt, insecure and feeling like I had no escape, I attempted suicide and landed in the hospital for three days. I took 20 of my grandmother's "Dexatrim" pills, bought a container of orange juice and swallowed them while I was on my way to school. I eventually told my cousin what I had done and she and a good friend took me to a local hospital for treatment.

They pumped my stomach, made me drink charcoal to detox my system and my family and a few friends came to the hospital. I recall my grandmother being upset and my grandfather standing over me crying his eyes out, but the rest of my family was unreactive and critical.

While hospitalized, my father and I were called in to speak to a psychologist because he was the root of my issues, but I was angry and he was unreceptive. When addressed, he said, "I'm her father and she needs to do what the fuck I say". The session was unsuccessful. I was subsequently released into my grandmother's custody and my father laid off the physical abuse for a few months.

My aunt referred to this incident as a "stunt for attention". Maybe it was, but not the way she insinuated. No one really took the time to understand where I was mentally. I didn't want to take my life, I was unhappy, unsure of myself and needed my circumstances to get better. I was crying out for help. My family moved on like nothing ever happened. I don't recall one conversation regarding why I would do something like that and we never followed up with a therapist as recommended.

"Fathers: Be your daughter's first love. Open doors for her, pull her seat out and talk to/treat her with the utmost respect...Set expectations on how a man should treat a

lady and she'll never settle for anything less".—Unknown

Months prior to my suicide attempt, I was dating a boy who visited me daily and occupied a lot of my time for a few months until I refused to sleep with him; I was 16 and still a virgin. Eventually, he moved on. I would pop up at his school, sweat him and he would tell me what I wanted to hear but, I knew he was seeing someone else. One day I popped up at his house and gave in to his wishes hoping it would rekindle our relationship.

My first sexual experience was not at all what it should have been. It took place on a sheet-less bed with someone I barely knew and didn't love, and it still didn't keep him around. To add insult to injury, he gave me an STD. My first time and he burned me. I couldn't go home to tell my grandmother or aunt because they didn't know I was having sex. A friend of mine took me to a local free clinic where I was diagnosed with "Trichomoniasis" and given seven pills to treat it. I didn't let anyone else touch me for months.

My daddy issues continued to fuel my need for attention from the opposite sex. I was attracted to much older men and began to secretly deal with a man on my block 10 years older and another from around the corner, six years older. I was sneaking to the 26 years old's house regularly, sleeping with him, and nobody in my family had a clue.

I knew I was out of order but I didn't care. He "liked"

me. The 22 year old would stop by my house occasionally and beep his horn for me to come outside. I would sneak off with him for a few hours without anyone knowing. I dealt with the two of them for months until they found out about each other.

Eventually, I started dating a guy closer to my age who was also a drug dealer, hanging with an unsavory group of friends, and gained exposure to alcohol, cigarettes and weed. My grades continued to falter and I was intensely truant. Socially, I hung tough with two girls, one in school and one at home, and visited my boyfriend across town the rest of the time. On weekends I would drink a 40 ounce of beer and take an occasional puff of a cigarette or weed just to fit in. I was never really a smoker and quickly strayed from it.

On a positive note, wanting to make my own money and have some of the nice things I saw my friends with, I filled out an application at a local Wendy's and was hired for my first part-time job. This gave me something constructive to do, exposed me to productive people and I excelled at it. I still avoided school though. My grandmother asked me daily if I went and I honestly told her I hadn't. School was a fashion show I didn't have the money to partake in and the overall environment didn't motivate me. It was not my scene.

I asked her numerous times to allow me to get my GED

and she refused. She was adamant I receive a high school diploma and she was right. When I missed enough school to hinder the teachers from grading me, my school guidance counselor contacted her for a meeting and made her aware of my attendance issues. Searching for a viable option, she agreed to withdraw me from school. I dropped out in the 11th grade and began attending a local alternative school to work toward my GED.

I attended school Monday through Thursday and took Fridays off to pick up my paycheck. My academic abilities were never the issue and after a month and a half of attending the school, I requested to sit for the GED exam. I passed on the first try with no formal plans moving forward. I spent the next few months sitting around during the day and working my part-time job in the evenings.

I really should have been doing something constructive during the day because sitting around the house just left the door open for drama. My house was pretty much a dictatorship. If you were a child, you didn't have a lot of say in the matter and <u>all</u> adults could tell you what to do, right or wrong. One day after an unnecessary argument with my uncle over dishes, my father yanked me by my hair and smacked me in the face over my refusal to apologize to my uncle. He never even asked my side of the story. Tired of the abuse, I hit him back and found myself on the dining room floor with him pounding on my

49

face. Two of my uncles stood there and watched, they always stood there and watched.

He continued to punch me and I continued to fight him back. I'm not sure how much time passed before he let me get up on my feet, but he followed me into my bedroom and began slapping me repeatedly, screaming "Say sorry! Say sorry!" I stood stubbornly until I couldn't take it anymore and finally yelled an apology in my uncle's direction. My face was severely bruised, I had a broken blood vessel in one eye and a busted lip from which I still wear a scar.

These incidents usually took place when my grandmother and aunt were out of the home. Still, nothing was ever done about it. My father saw it as discipline. After the incident was over I left the house for the day until my grandmother sent word with a friend that I could come home. My eye remained blood-shot for about a month and I walked around making up stories about why I looked that way.

One day he sent me to the store and once I returned, I screamed down the basement steps, "I'm back". He didn't say anything so I assumed he heard me. I went in the living room, called a friend and sat on the couch to have a conversation. Minutes later, he came upstairs, took the phone, hung it up, grabbed me by my arm, pulled me into the dining room and began slapping me in my face and slamming my head into the refrigerator. When I asked what I did, he said, "You didn't wait for my fucking response!" He was good for slapping me in my face and grabbing me by my hair when he put his hands on me. My hair seemed to be the first thing anyone reached for when I had any type of altercation. First chance I got, I cut it all off, I was sick of people using it as a weapon.

Another time, he entered my grandmother's room yelling at me for something ridiculous and I told him I hated him. He grabbed me, punched me in my face and pushed my upper body and head through my grandmother's bedroom window. She told me I had it coming because I shouldn't have told him I hated him.

The last abusive encounter happened because he didn't like something I said while he was excessively disciplining my younger sister. He hit me in my back with a weight belt, chased me into my aunt's room, grabbed me by my hair, and we began to fight. It was finally broken up by my aunt and grandmother. Once he cut me loose, I seized the opportunity and hit him repeatedly with a broom. He never hit me again. After the fight, my aunt called the police. They responded, got all sides of the story and even with my aunt's insistence that my father tended to be abusive, deducted that the matter was just a result of a parent disciplining their child.

When my father physically abused me, I felt like I was

one of the women I witnessed him beating as a child. There was no restraint. It was like he was taking some type of anger out on me. His method was certainly not discipline and there was no justification for him beating his child like that, no matter how angry he was.

After that last incident, I went to work a day later, didn't return home and refused to go back; I was 16 years old. My grandmother told my aunt (my uncle's ex-wife) what happened, she picked me up from a friend's house and offered to take me into her home. I am quite certain this caused her some issues with her husband who was not too fond of her continuing to have ties with my family but she took me anyway. Eventually, she asked her mother to take me in and she did for a few months but, I ended up back home with my grandmother. I never stayed away too long. Just like my time at boarding school, I was more drawn to dysfunction than peace and never wanted to be far from my grandmother.

When I returned home, the physical abuse remained in the past but left a huge scar. Besides his addiction and the stealing, those memories left me resentful and angry at my father for years. Progressively, those experiences also helped to shape the type of parent I would eventually be. Years later, when I became a mother, I had it set in my mind that spanking/beating would not be my go-to when disciplining my child.

I used alternative measures like time-out and did a lot of talking. I remembered being beaten or yelled at and not knowing why. I felt he wouldn't learn the lesson if he didn't understand what he did wrong. It worked because he never stayed angry and resentful toward me more than a day, and he always came back to apologize.

Still, I wasn't perfect, I was also a screamer in my parenting and could see the horror in his face when I yelled at him. He would shut down immediately. I always got better results when I spoke to him calmly. I still don't believe spanking should be the first resort when disciplining your child. Most often the situation doesn't even warrant physical punishment. A loss of temper is not so much about what the child did as it is about the parent's impatience with the situation.

Each time my father was abusive, his mind was altered by some drug. He doesn't even remember the incidents. I've mentioned some of them over the years and he just looks at me horrified and apologizes profusely. He never beat me like that when he was sober. He was kind and gentle, normally a very mild and quiet man. But, back then, he was rarely sober. I cried out for help through rebellion for years. I lashed out, talked back, walked around with a chip on my shoulder and my family maintained I was the problematic one.

Out of high school and no longer working my part time

job, I was doing absolutely nothing with my life. My aunt's boyfriend at the time approached me and asked what my plan was. I shrugged my shoulders. He suggested I begin to look into colleges and told me about a private college in the city that offered a popular major of "Paralegal Studies". I was open to the idea even though I had lifelong dreams of becoming a teacher. I didn't verbalize that to him though, I just went with the flow. He made an appointment for the next Monday, we toured the school and I enrolled.

Thank God he cared that much to get me on track. Lord knows where I would be had he not given me a positive option. He helped me break a cycle as I became the first in my immediate family to go to college and earn a degree (my aunt also took some college courses and earned a Dental Assistant certificate).

All positive male influence came from people outside my immediate family. Another one of my aunt's former boyfriends was and still remains a positive pillar of support in my life. He was a listening ear, taught me how to drive, and gave me a lot of love and encouragement. He saw through the smoke screen my family tried to present.

Another family friend gave me my first babysitting job at the age of 13. I watched his daughter after school so he and his wife could work and it got me out of the house for a few hours. Another was influential in my choice of school for the pursuit of my Bachelor's degree. These four individuals were aware of my household dynamic, saw something great in me and tried to develop it; pushed me to do better and be better.

My grandmother was so happy I achieved some semblance of graduation from high school (My alternative school held a commencement ceremony for GED recipients that year so I was able to walk in cap and gown). She was adamant I be productive and succeed. She used to say, "You're a "brainiac", you don't have to learn to be a home-maker, you are going to be successful and have maids" and "with that mouth of yours, you need to be a lawyer".

She saw success in me before I ever saw it in myself and put me on a pedestal but we were limited in our resources. She never really mentioned college, probably because we really couldn't afford it, but now, I was seeking higher education and she did all she could to ensure I was able to secure funding. She was so proud every time she saw me walk down the aisle to receive a degree. I handed my degree case to her each time and she would say, "Ok, go get the next one".

As I matured and began to walk down a better path, the dynamic of my father-daughter relationship continued to be ever-changing. The tension began to mellow when I was pregnant with my son. The relationship was unique because although I have been disappointed and hurt by him the majority of my life, I loved him dearly, felt a loyalty to him and would do anything for him. To this day, I always try to see the best in him and would never let him fall. I love him unconditionally and have covered up occasional wrongdoing.

For a long time, our relationship was extremely co-dependent and he was cocky about me having his back. He bragged about how he could always come to me and I would be there. He still does, and to a certain extent, he's right. I want to protect him, sometimes from himself, even though I haven't always felt protected and valued by him.

His reliance on me caused resentment in some of my siblings. They used to tease, "Yeah, you're Daddy's number one, he always tells us to go to you if something goes wrong with him and you'll know what to do". They didn't realize the very thing they were resenting was a very big load to carry. As the oldest child, he held me to a higher standard, expected more from me and put me through a lot more. You tend to run to the person that will drop everything and run to your beck and call. There is nothing glamorous about living in the role of caretaker when in some ways, you need to be taken care of.

Despite, I give my father credit for times he would get himself together, if only for a day, in order to support me in my important moments (i.e.: graduations, religious ceremonies etc.). He'd sober himself up, shower, shave and participate in the days' activities. He'd get high later that night but he was present physically and mentally for a few hours.

My mother was present for one of my college graduations as well and was instrumental in finding financial resources to assist me in returning to college to pursue my Bachelor's degree. I had previously defaulted on a student loan and could not secure the funding myself. She also made an effort to bond with my son when he was little. I allowed her to spend time with him a few times and she was very kind to him; I appreciated that. I like to give credit where credit is due because, I believe we all have exceptional moments worthy of acknowledgment.

Today, through growth and him entering recovery, my relationship with my father has been able to find complete healing, mostly because of his willingness to be accountable for his actions. I can talk to him about anything and we've definitely had some very difficult discussions, but he has always heard me out, never invalidates my feelings and never judges me. His response to a recent conversation was, *"Baby girl, I listened to you last night and all I can say is I don't remember any of the things you said I did. I don't know how you would even want me to still be part of your life. Damn, I was a monster. I'm so sorry for what I put you through"*.

Statements like this have facilitated healing and forgiveness. His actions have yielded an apology and best of all atonement.

He has also made up for the past through his interaction and bonding with my son. Often times, he attended his sporting events, worked with him on his basketball, ran him to McDonald's when I wouldn't and even made himself available for parent/teacher conferences (that was good as gold for me). He has also shown understanding when I lashed out and sometimes said very mean things.

Our relationship is not without flaw but we love and support each other to the best of our abilities. We're in tune with each other emotionally and I'm not angry with him anymore. I still get disappointed sometimes because he has his struggles but I'm not angry. I know he loves me and his issues were not about me.

I had a very recent conversation with my mother and I can imagine how hard it was for her to hear my thoughts and feelings, but she finally apologized for failing to uphold her parental responsibilities. That single conversation added about 10 years to my life. I've been walking around pissed for 44 years but now I feel I can gain the capacity to forgive. I still need her to respect my boundaries and understand I already hold a mother/daughter bond with my grandmother and nothing will ever trump that. I don't always agree with some of the things she says but, I can agree to disagree and move forward from here. Thank God for healing.

"The art of healing comes from nature and not the physician. Therefore, the physician must start from nature with an open mind"—Paraclesus

Other Female Perspectives...

To gain further perspective and show a commonality, I have taken a survey involving several participants willing to share their experiences involving the absence or broken relationship with a parent.

1. Please provide a brief synopsis of the circumstances behind the parental absence

My father was a career criminal and for most of my life was an alcoholic or drug abuser. Most of my memories of my father hold some sort of painful or harmful experience that negatively impacted my childhood. **-E.B.-Maryland**

My mother *was strung out on drugs and involved in prostitution which made her absent from my life willingly and unwillingly.* ***My dad*** *was strung out on drugs most of my life, cleaned up, struggled some more and now goes through spells as the addiction changed from drugs to alcohol.* **-A.G.-Maryland**

My mother was addicted to heroin since I was 4 years old. She left me to be raised by my great grandparents. **-M.F.-Maryland**

For the most part, my dad was a sweet, honest (when not on drugs) and loving man. Never really showed much affection but, I knew he loved me. I remember him teaching me how to ride my bike and how he was there for me when I was about to have my first fight. Taught me how to stand up for myself. In his words "Ain't no punks around here" lol. But, I was around the age of five when my dad became addicted to crack. I lived with my mom, stepdad and two younger brothers in Brooklyn. My dad lived with my grandparents in Queens.

Every weekend, every year during the entire summer or

whenever I did not have school we would be in Queens with my dad and grandparents. Sometimes, my dad would disappear for days or maybe even weeks. My friends and I would ride our bikes or scooters up to Guy R. Brewer Blvd or Farmers Blvd to see if we saw him standing outside. If I saw him I would tell him to go home and of course he would lie and say I'm coming. (Discovered at a later age, those were crack binges). He was in and out of jail most of my teenage years and young adult life. He missed out on my H.S. Graduation. **-S.H.-New York**

My birth mother, due to an ongoing battle with addiction to crack cocaine was never really present in my life. I'm not sure when or if she ever went into rehab; it is my understanding that she still struggles with addiction to this day. My father was present in the beginning but, also struggled with addiction to crack cocaine until I was three years old. He entered rehab and wasn't super prominent in my life for a few years. My aunt was my primary caretaker until the age of 10 or 11. **-D.W.-North Carolina**

My mother was absent due to her being addicted to heroin. My father used to sell drugs and later became addicted as well; he was constantly in and out of prison. As a result, neither one of my parents were there to physically raise me. My great grandmother was the one who brought me home from the hospital and raised me due to their circumstances. I was born addicted to heroin. **-I.J.-Maryland**

Both of my parents have had some issues that prevented them from being present. My mom turned to drugs and my dad was caught up in the streets which caused him to spend a lot of time in jail and away from us. **-U.S.-Georgia**

2. What (if any) psychological damage/trauma did you incur as a result of this experience? How did it affect your development?

My father's absence negatively affected my identity as a child and my self-worth as both a child and an adult. I often tried to be the smartest student and achieve a lot of success to overcompensate for my lack of self-worth. **-E.B.-Maryland**

The damage incurred by my father was physical, verbal and emotional abuse. The damage from my mother was abandonment. When I was younger, I thought of ending my life often because I felt like if that was how life was always going to be it wasn't worth living. It tainted the strength I never knew I had because I was never told I was someone special, someone worth more than what I could do for someone. Abuse was used to keep me at the mentality of just being good enough to breathe the same air as my father. I was what people wanted me to be. To some extent, I still am. If I use my voice, there are people that try to stifle me and think it is okay.

I would have rather felt nothing for many years than to deal with even a little bit of pain and for a good portion of my teen years and twenties, I did feel nothing. It seemed like the best way to avoid pain and honestly did help me cope with any pain thrown my way. I started to be able to dissect situations that applied to me versus the ones that didn't.

I emotionally detached myself from feeling for other people, mostly because I didn't want to anymore. Taking other people's feelings into consideration was how I was trained to be, so it was supposed to be important. It became unimportant to me. I was the only one who cared about my feelings. It wasn't until I was exposed to innocent love, my nieces and nephews and my first born child, that I allowed myself to receive genuine love. It was really hard and can be a struggle at times but it is the best feeling to know that there is someone who could truly love you with no expectations other than being given love in return. **-A.G.- Maryland**

My mother's addiction left me feeling abandoned. As a child I always felt like I wasn't good enough. I always had to accept getting less than I was worth. Even when it came to small things like eating dinner, I received less food on my plate than the other kids. From that point on, I never felt worthy. **-M.F.- Maryland**

As far as it affecting me, I think it played a part in me dealing with older men and having a child at 16. It also played a part in me growing up fast. It was easier for me to communicate by having sex than actually having a conversation. I was young and naïve and thought I knew it all. **-S.H.-New York**

I feel in some ways that people have ulterior motives when it comes to befriending me or taking any interest in me at all; I always feel like I am being used to make someone jealous or as an ego booster. I never feel like there is genuine interest in me. I also tend to make myself smaller so that I am not noticed; trying not to cause a scene. For example: once, when I was a child, I was supposed to visit my birth mother and I told my aunt and father I didn't want to go anymore. I felt torn and like a pawn in a game I really didn't want to play. My birth mother caused a scene, started screaming, "That's my daughter too! This is my weekend!". At this point, she had one arm and my aunt had the other like they were playing tug of war. I remember crying but, nobody seemed to hear me. I feel like maybe, my life could have been a bit different if my biological parents were able to parent me together. -D.W.-North Carolina

It affected my development because, I used to wonder why other children were lucky enough to have their parents, and I didn't. I wanted my mother and father to raise me; I felt let down and hurt. There wasn't anything I needed per se or anything that I didn't have, I just wanted my parents be a part of my life. My great grandmother did a phenomenal job and I couldn't have asked for anyone better. She gave me all the love that a child could want for.

My parents being mostly absent from my life made me act out to get attention. I used to get angry and become withdrawn when they made promises to come and see me and wouldn't show up. The broken promises would take me through something terrible emotionally. My great grandmother was the one who unfortunately had to deal with my disposition at the time. It made me lash out and become unruly. My great grandmother saw fit to put me in counseling so that I would be able to deal with my feelings but, I didn't change overnight.

As a matter of fact, I stayed in counseling for several years as a child. Counseling helped me to deal with my feelings appropriately. When the counselor determined that a lot of the reason for my behavior was due to my parents broken promises, my great grandmother tried to talk to my father and even had him come to a therapy session; he didn't change.

My mother would stay away from her family while addicted to heroin because she didn't want us to see her that way. My great grandmother decided to allow me to see my parents only after it was cleared through her. She used to allow me to go with them and give them a certain time to return me home but, after she saw the effects of their inconsistency, she stopped that. I was only allowed to see them if they came to the house to see me. - **I.J.-Maryland**

*I have a hard time trusting and believing people but, when I do, I become attached; which isn't always good or healthy. For a long time, I attracted guys similar to my dad; the street, thuggish type. That didn't work out too well for me. I also feel I became hardened and a bit selfish, which was a direct result of lies and hurt. -***U.S.-Georgia**

3. Please describe any role reversals that took place in your family as a result of the experience.

*My father did not provide financially for myself or my brother. As a young adult, I began to assist my mother in providing financially for my brother. I essentially became a parent at the age of 18 to a child that I did not birth. -***E.B.-Maryland**

*My grandmother raised me along with my paternal aunt, I know my aunt as my mother. She too is emotionally abusive though. In some shape or form I think everyone in our family has been verbally abusive at one point or another. You learn from the environment you are raised in. I was dubbed the "mother hen" because I took care of everyone. I had a lot of responsibility and was responsible for every person younger than me. It was a heavy weight on my shoulders and I resented them and anyone older than me because it was my weight. As an adult, I have a better relationship with the sibling/cousin clan that I was raised with but as a kid, I was very resentful. I regret that now and hope as an adult that I made amends for anything that I've done to hurt them.-***A.G.-Maryland**

As a result of my Mother's addiction, I always felt like I had to take care of her. I thought if I didn't take care of her, she would abandon me all over again, like she did when I was younger. I felt like I wasn't good enough to be My Mother's child and I was the reason she was an addict. I'm still raising my Mother's kids, taking the responsibility from her and accepting her abusive ways. **-M.F.-Maryland**

Because of my dad's addiction, my grandparents took on a lot of his responsibilities. They were with me until the age of 14. When he went missing, they would have their tenant come and get us from Brooklyn. While they were alive, they made sure we had a great childhood. I grew up a spoiled brat; maybe my grandparents spoiled me because they were trying to make up for what my dad didn't do. I believe that if my grandparents didn't die when I was 14 years old, I wouldn't have lost my virginity. **-S.H.-New York**

My aunt and grandmother were basically my mom until my dad cleaned up and got together with my stepmother and she took on the role. **-D.W.-North Carolina**

My great-grandmother raised me. I also have a sister but, we were not raised in the same household; she was raised by our other great-grandmother. Later in life, my mother had another daughter who was adopted due to there being no one else in the family to raise her. **-I.J.-Maryland**

My paternal grandparents raised my sister and I, as well as some of our cousins. Once my mom turned to drugs, she lost everything; even her three youngest kids. I fought to get them out of the system and out of stranger's homes and, I eventually won in 2009; I have had them ever since. They jokingly call me "sis-mom". **-U.S.-Georgia**

4. How did the experience directly affect your ability to form healthy relationships (parents, friends and intimate partners)? Please explain

A lack of love and care tremendously affected my ability to have a healthy romantic relationship. I did not understand how a man should love or treat me because I never had an example of that from my father. I suffer from abandonment anxiety in my relationships because I fear my partner will leave me and it will be as devastating as it was every time my father was arrested or relapsed. **-E.B.-Maryland**

Friends & Family: *Every relationship <u>except</u> friendships were hard to maintain. Most of my friends were a sure thing. I did really well choosing them. They got to really know me. My immediate family was not always a sure thing. Most of them still don't know who I really am; for a long time, I didn't know me. I learned to cope with each person individually and it wasn't always easy. I was the person people took stuff out on. Some people still see me as the kid they knew.*

Intimate partners: *It was easy getting involved in a relationship. A spade could call a spade, but it wasn't easy choosing someone I wanted to stick around for the long haul. I was usually the person who didn't want to stick around. It wasn't because the bar was set too high, it was because I wasn't ready to have another adult depend on me for anything, even intimacy. Relationships are hard in general but if you've taken verbal abuse off of your family, you become defensive and everything your partner says could be interpreted as abusive. It's all about the tone of voice you say something, it can all be misleading. I was pretty content with not being attached to anyone until about 2 years ago when someone showed me that I was worth it.* **-A.G.-**

Maryland

My mother's addiction affected my ability to form healthy relationships because I have trust issues. I always feel afraid to let people get too close to me. I feel like I have to hide from people because my mother used to hide from me. My mother used to leave me late at night by myself and I would wake up in the middle of the night crying my eyes out. I feel like everyone will leave me hurt so, I keep my distance. **-M.F.-Maryland**

Today, I have a really great relationship with my dad. I speak to him every day or every other day. I am not mad at him for the things he has done in the past. As I grew up and learned that he was on drugs, I always felt that underneath the drug addiction, he was a great guy. I think because I look at my dad that way, it played a part when dealing with intimate partners. Sometimes I excused their behavior, feeling that I understood where they were coming from. But, not realizing that I deserve better. Because my dad is not affectionate, I am also not affectionate. - **S.H.-New York**

I have a hard time developing platonic friendships with women. I find that I always approach in a sexual manner and always, somehow look for validation from them. I didn't realize until I got to my adult years that I was looking for my mother in these women. Although my stepmother was in my life from the time I was about four, I still felt a void for the tenderness I never got from my birth mother. I wondered, why didn't she want me? I don't hold any animosity toward her as I understand that addiction is a choice but, once it takes hold of you, you have no control. But, it still hurt me. **-D.W.-North Carolina**

It affected my ability to form healthy relationships because I was willing to give more than I received. Deep down inside, I felt

68

that a potential partner would abandon me as my parents had done. I have also been the type to write people off if they say or do something that I didn't like, for fear of getting hurt. Trust, is a big thing for me. I will give a person the benefit of the doubt at first, but once I feel betrayed, a whole different person emerges.

It has affected me in ways that I didn't even know existed until I sat down and examined myself. I would rather hurt someone before they hurt me. **-I.J.-Maryland**

As I previously mentioned, it is extremely hard for me to trust people and believe the things they say or promise. I don't believe people when they say they love and care for me (friends, family, significant other etc.). It's like I'm always waiting for the other shoe to drop because, most often, I know it will. **-U.S.-Georgia**

5. What measures have you taken to break any unhealthy cycles?

- *I have attended therapy for almost four years to gain knowledge about how I can practice positive self-talk and improve my lack of love for myself.*
- *I have learned how to establish healthy boundaries in all of my relationships to eliminate co-dependent relationships.*
- *I have forgiven my father for his absence in my life and made peace with his death*

-E.B.-Maryland

- *I forgave my parents. Forgiving my mother was easier; she had to live with her mistakes and suffered for the choices that she made all the time. In my adult years, she just wanted to be in my life and have a relationship with her*

69

grandchildren. I made amends with her before her passing and miss her dearly; she became my best friend. As for my father, I have forgiven him but, I have also accepted that there are things about him that will never change. Certain mannerisms of his are still a trigger for me but, I don't think he's a bad person. I don't try to meet his expectations anymore.

- *I forgave myself.* I realized that my parent's choices were not my fault. I was told I was at fault for a long time and I believed it; I took the time to find out who I was and what I wanted out of life.

- *I sought counseling.* Counseling saved my life. I would not be here if I didn't seek it. I was in and out of counseling since the third grade and each time, it saved a part of my sanity.

- *Relocation.* I was relocated by my sister and it helped me heal. Having a good example of how to live independently was a breath of fresh air. Seeing someone set goals and meet them and strive for better was what I needed in my life. I will always be thankful to her because she saved a part of me that would have been lost.

- *Love and Live.* I learned to love myself and others; give and receive. I learned to let things go. I have one life to live and I live it. I do what makes me happy and I fight for what I want. I believe in myself and know I will succeed. I validate myself because nobody can do that better than me. **-A.G.-Maryland**

I heal the pain of my past by giving myself the love that I didn't receive from my Mother. I make sure that I'm here for my four children by making sure they feel loved and protected. I'm married to my best friend and we show our children a great example of love, friendship and compassion *for others. I believe when you keep God first you can heal through any bad situation.-**M.F.-Maryland***

*First step I took to get myself together was reading the Bible. It helped me to heal and improve myself. I have forgiven. I understand my purpose. I am comfortable with being who I am and learning to not always have negative thoughts. I speak up for myself when necessary. And, have love and respect for myself and others. I still need to work on being affectionate. -**S.H.-New York***

I am more conscious of the way I deal with or approach women. I have also been doing some self-reflection, meditation and other self-exploring activities. I vow to never and will take certain steps to ensure that I never put any children I may have through the same things I experienced as a child, with regard to an absent, substance abused parent. **-D.W.-North Carolina**

Being an adult and being fully aware of the type of heart I have, beautiful spirit and all my flaws, I'm very open with people from the very beginning so that we both know what we expect from each other. I'll even share my past with a person if I feel that we're going in the direction of becoming serious, so they will know and understand the type of person they're dealing with and they can decide whether they want to be a part of my world. I have found that being upfront is the best way to go. There are probably things that I'll still learn about myself as time goes on but, this is it for now. I also do the following:

1. Pray

2. *Counseling helped me tremendously as a child; it probably wouldn't be a bad idea to revisit it.*

3. *Keeping my heart in-tact **-I.J.-Maryland***

*As I grow older, I have been taking steps to heal as I become more aware of my issues. The biggest part of my growth has been "understanding". I try to understand people so I can eventually gain clarity on what motivates them to be the way they are and do the things they do. I stay away from hard drugs (I do smoke weed). I always do my best to say what I mean and mean what I say. I make sure that my word counts. I give the benefit of the doubt and second chances, if deserved. I do my best to be there for my loved ones, no matter what. I strive to be honest, loyal, genuine, caring and kind-hearted every day of my life. I remain aware and choose my company wisely so I don't fall into the traps that my parents did. **-U.S.-Georgia***

A Male Perspective...

1. Please provide a brief synopsis of the circumstances behind the parental absence

   My father was not in my life so, I didn't have male structure in the home. My mother was addicted to drugs and we were living in the projects where about 75% percent of the people were going through the same thing so, that took her out of the home. -M.V.-New Jersey

2. What (if any) psychological damage/trauma did you incur as a result of this experience? How did it affect your development?

   I had to learn how to be a man by myself because there were only women in my immediate family. When you're a kid and don't understand what's happening, you feel alone. I heard I love you but, questioned it. All of this affected my development and I became rebellious because none of them were my beautiful, loving mother that I kept in my mind and heart -M.V.-New Jersey

3. Please describe any role reversals that took place in your family as a result of the experience.

   My aunts became mother figures. Although there was family there to help, I had to look after my sibling; I felt like I had to be her dad even though it wasn't asked of me. Looking out for her became second nature to me as I still tried to be a "child". -M.V.-New Jersey

4. How did the experience directly affect your ability to form
    healthy relationships (parents, friends and intimate
    partners)? Please explain

    *I love my mother to death. We are great because
    conversations were had at every visit and during every phone
    call from day one, to let me know I wasn't abandoned.*

    *I barely have any friends. I turn to people I hold dear in my
    extended family. I am very guarded in my life, I am the
    "rock" of the family. If I'm hurting, you won't know; I'm
    introverted.*

    *With intimate partners, it is very hard. I don't know how to
    express love and affection as I should and that caused me to
    lose a lot of good relationships. I've been too proud to ask
    for guidance on how to act with women and sometimes kids.*
    -M.V.-New Jersey

5. What measures have you taken to break any unhealthy
    cycles?

    - *I speak with people about "regular life"; family included
      and work daily to be better, learn to love and be humble.*
    - *I am allowing myself to be vulnerable sometimes so my
      kids will never know that type of hurt or sense of loss.*

    *I am far from perfect and, I am still learning to find healing
    but, I am getting there slowly but, surely with the help of
    others (whether they know it or not). It is a process. I don't
    trust many people so, professional help is a no-go for me; I
    tried it as a child.*

    -M.V.-New Jersey

From the Perspective of a Once Addicted/ Absentee Parent
L.C. - North Carolina

1. Please provide a brief synopsis of the circumstances behind your absence

   I was addicted to crack cocaine. My addiction started from curiosity. I had a great upbringing; I did not need for anything. I was actually a spoiled child and had a lot of advantages my older siblings did not have growing up with our very strict and old fashioned parents.

2. What (if any) psychological damage/trauma did you or your children incur as a result of this experience? How did it affect their development?

   The most hurtful thing for me was putting my family through a lot of worry. My children, especially my son was traumatized by having to be removed from my care due to my addiction when a report was made and strangers came to take them away. I also placed them and my mom (who suffered from Alzheimer's) in danger by leaving them alone and unattended.

3. Please describe any role reversals that took place in your family as a result of the experience.

   My sister took responsibility for my children with assistance from my sister-in-law and her children; they took great care of them. As I look back, my son had a hard time. He was rebellious and gave my sister a hard time. She continued to

75

do right by him but, I know it was a little too much for her to handle; especially with my mom's condition.

4. How did the experience directly affect your ability to form healthy relationships with your children/family? Please explain

Building a relationship with my children once I went through treatment, established a career and found a suitable place to live was challenging. I had to remember what I did to cause them to be removed from my care. Even though they were extremely happy to be with me again, I can't help but wonder if they felt safe and secure; they never said otherwise.

My relationship with my sister was a little work at first. I needed to prove to her, as well as myself that the life I was living was in the past and was a lesson learned. I had to rebuild trust with her and the rest of my family.

5. What measures have you taken to break any unhealthy cycles?

You must abstain from negative people, places and things is what we were taught going through recovery. I never returned to those old places except my family home in order to say goodbye to my mom. Once we buried her that was the last time I went to that neighborhood.

The Loss of My Brother...

I wish to posthumously discuss my brother based on our personal conversations and my own personal perspective. He's not here to speak for himself but I believe his journey is essential to this book as well.

My brother and I were four years apart (I'm the oldest) but, he was the closest thing I had to a twin. We had a language all our own, were connected at the heart and bonded through trauma; we called each other "Sissy" and "Bubba". We fought like any other siblings but we were tight.

I understood him and his pain. He was always his authentic self and very transparent with me because he knew I accepted and loved him good, bad or indifferent. He extended the same unconditional love to me.

As a young child, he was spoiled but innocent and wouldn't hurt a fly. As he grew, he developed a deep sadness he didn't reveal to many. He had voids, trauma, insecurities, feelings of indebtedness, depression, anger and a heart that screamed out for love.

He also experienced absent and addicted parents. Our father was addicted for the greater part of his

77

life and mostly absent. He was angry at him for not being there and they had a tumultuous relationship for years. Fortunately they were able to reach a common ground as my brother entered adulthood.

His mother was addicted for a number of years during his adolescence but, she always loved, doted on him and tried to give him the world. He loved her and would do anything for her as well. The relationship was also co-dependent and a bit suffocating for him at times.

Although he spent the majority of his life with his mother, he always found his way back to us. He lived with us around the age of six or seven, taken care of by our grandmother and aunt until he was relocated to another state. He ran away from home and came back to us at the age of 15. Thereafter, he was back and forth between the two into adulthood.

In his teens, he began to experiment with marijuana and alcohol and eventually moved on to recreationally use harder drugs to medicate himself. The more he became unable to cope with his voids, the angrier he got and began to change. He became involved with the wrong types of people, developed a very cold demeanor and turned to the streets. He loved his family but was only close to a few.

He didn't talk much but, was intelligent, well-spoken and well-written. He was also artistic (he loved to draw), intrigued by music and athletically inclined. His greatest talents were overshadowed by the false persona he felt obligated to offer the world. There were people around him every day that didn't know the real him. To them, he was a gun toting, hardcore dude that wasn't to be played with. He was the "muscle" they ran to when they needed help with a beef. Even in his new demeanor, he never looked for trouble.

I watched him struggle to form meaningful friendships (he had a few) and bond in a healthy manner with intimate partners as he didn't trust many people. He had girlfriends but, relationships were not his priority. He eventually became the father of three children who he loved but also struggled to bond with.

He would often tell me how he expected his lifestyle to catch up with him and eventually, it led to a stint in prison where he began to reflect and make positive changes. He used his time to focus on fitness and worked toward his GED.

Upon release, he was diligent about continuing on a productive path. He was involved in a healthy relationship and enrolled in college where his talents emerged and he excelled. He also began drawing again. He was setting goals and planned to embark on some entrepreneurial opportunities. He was optimistic about the future but he still had his demons: drinking and recreational drug use.

We lived in different states so we didn't see each other much but, when we did, we picked up where we left off. We would sit and talk for hours, clearing out the difficult areas that we could only share with each other.

The last time I saw him, we were sitting at my uncle's dining room table discussing his college experience. He was telling me about a school project he was working on and his goals for the future. We ended our meeting with a "see you later" because we planned to meet at his mother's house for dinner that evening. Because of that, I didn't hug and kiss him goodbye. I showed up to the dinner but he didn't. That was the last time I saw him alive. The vices he developed over the years claimed his life at the age of 35 when he died of an accidental overdose.

When notified of his death, I was beside myself with grief. I was given two stories regarding the cause until I was finally told the correct one. All I could think about was how great he looked and sounded when I saw him 11 days prior. I couldn't wrap my mind around it; I still can't.

At a concert when I was notified, I exited the venue and quickly ran to my sister's house to be with my family. We departed for his home state at the end of the week; his funeral was on a Friday. While attending the viewing, I held my niece's hand, trembling as I walked toward his casket.

When I caught the first glimpse of his body, I immediately began to hover over him and look for small pieces of evidence that it was him (i.e. scars on his cheek and eyebrow). He did not look at all like himself. My loved ones assured me that it was him. I began to scream and cry, wrapped my arms around him and tried to pull his body out of the casket. In my mind, I needed him to wake up so this nightmare could be over.

He had a beautiful funeral service and repast with lots of family and friends in attendance but eventually, it was time to make my journey home. I struggled knowing that every trip I would take to that state in the future would be void of his presence. I was used to him immediately running to my side when he knew I was in town.

I got home and delved back into work. I worked, went home, went to bed at 6 pm every evening and shut everyone out, except my son and husband. There are five stages of grief and I went through each one. To this day, I have never seen the autopsy report because I just can't handle it.

For the first two years following his death, I would visit his home state and get an anxious feeling as soon as I crossed the state line because I knew I wasn't going to see him. I would go to his mother's house, pick up his urn, cradle it in my arms and weep. I just didn't want to believe or accept it. He was getting his life on track. He had a bright future ahead and now, he was gone.

I was so overcome with anger and denial, I constantly posted pictures of him on social media. I didn't want his presence to go away and wanted everyone else to remember him too. I questioned God; he was getting it right, why did you take him? I vehemently scolded myself: "He never lied to you about his vices, you knew everything about him, did you miss something? Why didn't you hug him and tell him you loved him before he left that day?"

I was so deeply saddened and debilitated by this loss the mere mention of his name reduced me to tears; it still does. At my lowest point, he came to me in a dream telling me he had to go away but, I needed to continue to live. That's when I started to snap out of it a bit. The dream was so vivid I could feel him sitting next to me.

I believe his struggles were a direct result of his inability to cope with the trauma and hurt he had inside. His death is by far one of the greatest losses I have ever suffered and greatest pain I have ever felt. The experience taught me how important it is to look deeper and listen closer. You can be so close to someone and still have things left unsaid.

My life was blessed because my brother was part of it. His remains are now resting peacefully at a beautiful memorial park facing a tree and body of water; a place I chose for him. I will love him for the rest of my life and have peace knowing he has nothing but happiness now.

L.M.H. 12/14/1978-7/17/2014

Forever in my Heart

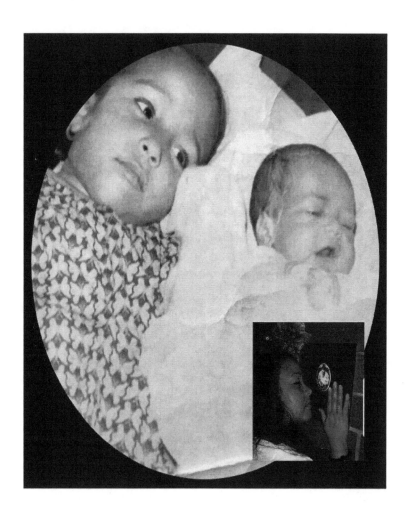

CHAPTER 3

College, True Love and Teen Parenting

I started college in the middle of spring, 1992, was on a constructive track academically, making respectable friends and traveling outside of my town and borough. My world was opening up and I had my first exposure to Greek organizations (sororities and fraternities). I was thriving and definitely in my element.

I was pursuing an Associate's degree, spent a lot of time in the school library honing my study habits and came out the gate my first semester with a 3.8 GPA. I wasn't sure if I liked my major but I was finishing what I started. I would often leave home bright and early in the morning and remain in the city hours after school let out. I loved to sit in Grand Central Station and watch the people walk by or walk up 42nd Street to Times Square just to be in the heart of it. It gave me peace.

By the time my second quarter hit, I had made a few friends and become enthralled with Greek and party life. My grades began to suffer a bit but I was still above water. During this time, I met a guy enrolled in the same program. He was originally from Harlem, was the cool dude in school, had lots of friends, and all the girls liked him. Two years older than me, he had chocolate skin, a big, beautiful smile, was soft spoken and an all-around nice guy. I was captivated from afar, but he had a girlfriend and I was respectful of his status. I also had a boyfriend in Queens.

Through our affiliations with the school fraternity and sorority, in passing, and after he came to a party I threw, I became further acquainted with him and two other guys from the school. All three lived in my borough and we began to connect on that commonality. I became so cool with them they often stopped by my house on weekends to visit. We sat outside for hours, talking and laughing and became fast friends.

One day, they stopped by and asked if I would be interested in going to a local park with them and I agreed. While hanging in the park, the cute guy and I began to connect on a deeper level. He pushed me on the swing for hours while we talked about life, goals and his aspirations to become a police officer. During the conversation, I asked him what was up with his girlfriend and he said they had decided to take a "break".

I believed what he said and soon after, he began to spend an exorbitant amount of time with me, especially after school hours. Our other friend used to park his car in front of cutie's house so he'd drive to my house after school and we'd sit and talk for hours, sometimes into the middle of the night. I had an idea that either his "ex" wasn't completely over him or he wasn't giving me the full story as she would beep him frequently. I never questioned it though.

We continued to see each other discreetly in school and freely outside because he said he didn't want to rub our relationship in her face. Once word got out, I became known as the "homewrecker". How was I a homewrecker? He told me they weren't together anymore. I soon discovered although they agreed to take a "break", they were not on the same page regarding possible reconciliation.

This girl maintained close ties with his family and had them all thinking I stole her boyfriend. She even attended a family function after he and I became official. I confronted him, asked for the truth and he stubbornly insisted it was over between the two of them. I insisted if he was telling me the truth, he needed to make it clear to her. Shortly thereafter, he went to the girl and told her there was no chance of reconciliation. From then on, we were together in the open.

We remained inseparable, spent every waking moment together, and I fell deeply in love with him. He was a great addition to my life and my family loved him. He was ambitious, productive, kind, giving, affectionate, fun and he liked me for ME. Wanting nothing but my time, he was different and that sometimes made me uncomfortable. We had limited money but we went on dates, took pictures at "Moto photo" in Green Acres Mall, went to church together, and he regularly gave me flowers, cards and greatest of all, RESPECT.

After months of spending every minute together our relationship began to take a turn. I began spending a lot of time at a local Army recruitment center and less time with him. I set my sights on going into the military and was considering dropping out of school to do it. I was still grasping for straws, trying to find direction.

He wasn't happy about this plan as he knew it would take me away from him. We began to butt heads but, we loved each other and continued to work through it. Six months after we began dating, I missed a period. I went to my aunt's boyfriend (the one who enrolled me in the school) and confided that I suspected I might be pregnant. He agreed not to tell.

I snuck my grandmother's insurance card out of her purse and went to Planned Parenthood to be tested. My suspicions were confirmed and after sonogram, they informed me I was 8 weeks pregnant. I told my boyfriend, he asked me what I wanted to do and we decided to keep the baby.

I'd gotten pretty far in the military process, sworn in and

had even been given my Basic Training and Advanced Individual Training locations but I ran into some technical difficulties with my school's credentialing. While they were looking into that, I found out I was pregnant, so that would have to go on hold anyway.

I was afraid to tell my family the news and hid it for as long as I could. I told my aunt's ex-boyfriend first and then my father who I thought would flip but, was calm and supportive. I eventually told my grandmother who began to suggest I consider terminating the pregnancy. She even used a tactic of telling me my grandfather would stop speaking to me if I decided to have a baby at my age, he later negated that statement. I never told my aunt, I was too scared. She called me to her room one day, asked if I was pregnant and I confirmed it.

She told me she knew because my body had begun to change and every time I came to have a conversation with her, I hid my body behind the door. She was calm at first but eventually began to aggressively urge me to abort. She went as far as trying to coerce my boyfriend to side with her by telling him "I didn't need to have a baby because I didn't even want to take care of my own siblings". He didn't listen and abortion was never an option for me anyway. She eventually got on board when I hit the five month mark and was extremely supportive for the rest of my pregnancy. She gave me one of three baby showers and ran back and forth to the hospital with me during false and active labor. I also chose her to be one of my baby's godmothers.

I looked forward to the birth of my baby and immediately set it in my mind that I would be everything my parents weren't to me. I was going to set good examples and be the best mother ever. My baby wasn't going to have the voids I had. In my youth there were plenty of family members telling me how I should conduct my life without setting any good example.

I was 18 years old and high-risk pregnant because of the stress at home but, I remained in school and was determined to graduate. I was also unemployed, clueless and winging it day by day. I attended school at night and worked an Internship during the day with my boyfriend's support. We <u>both</u> graduated with our degrees.

Three months after graduation, I gave birth to a healthy baby boy via C-section and my life changed. My Son gave me air in my lungs. For the first year we were a cohesive family, maintaining a healthy circle of friends and doing well sharing the responsibility of caring for our little boy.

His father was very hands-on and my heart was full but reality was, we were broke. My boyfriend was working a part-time security job paying approximately $200 per week and I was unemployed so I could be home to take care of our son.

He provided for us the best he could. He never bought a thing for himself without making sure we had something too. I began charging up credit cards issued to me as a college graduate in an effort to do my part. I also collected welfare and food stamps. I was destroying my credit by the day but was contributing to the care of our son. He acquired the same debt increasing habits.

(Mommy and Torey (seven months old) - 4[h] of July at South Street Seaport with Dad)

I continued to live at home with my family, hoping for a way out, with no clue how to execute. My boyfriend eventually secured an opportunity for us to acquire our own apartment through his godfather who had several units for rent. You'd think I would jump at the opportunity as it would get me out of my family home and into my own but I declined. It meant moving uptown to Harlem and as much as I hated the dysfunction in my house, I was equally scared to leave the nest and my grandmother. I was still a kid myself so, my boyfriend didn't push the issue and we continued to live separately with occasional sleepovers at each other's houses.

Essentially, I began to sabotage the relationship. I complained about stupid things and started petty arguments. His mother was not fond of me from the beginning and made a lot of false assumptions about me without giving me a fair chance. He also made me aware that several of his family members had called me "stuck up and standoffish" and that made me want to shy away even more. Eventually, I did build a close bond with several of them, especially his sister.

Still, I wanted a good relationship with his mother because I loved her son and felt it was important. Her rejection and reluctance to get to know me hurt and I clung to any positive interaction I had with her with hopes that we could build a bond. She was cordial to me but the close bond didn't happen and that was hard for me as an already insecure 19 year old. Years later, I even wrote her a letter expressing my feelings and had a subsequent conversation with her. During the exchange, she told me back then, she felt I was spoiled, selfish and superficial. I respected her feedback but still felt she never took the time to look into my heart.

I accused him of never enlightening his mom about who I really was. I felt he was too passive and didn't protect me and I resented that. The more I complained, the more he made light of the situation telling me all that mattered was how he felt about me. At the end of the day, he was right because he was the one I had to maintain a healthy relationship with but I needed him to understand my position as well.

To get his attention, I began to cheat on him with someone I cared nothing about. That person gave me what I was used to: talked to me like I was shit, used me for sex and didn't give a damn about me....That was familiar!

My boyfriend found out about my indiscretion and confronted me but didn't leave. He tried his best to work through it and in the end took a chance on his love for me and gave me an engagement ring. I accepted his proposal and started to get my act together.

I still had a desire to enter the military and began seeing a recruiter again but now, I had a few strikes against me. I was holding some of the pregnancy weight and since I was technically unmarried, would have to sign over custody of my son to a caretaker. I was absolutely unwilling to do that.

In turn, my boyfriend met with my recruiter and decided to enter the Army. His plan was to make a better life for us and our son and I was on board. He departed for basic training a month after our son's first birthday. I supported him through the new endeavor, traveled to attend his graduation and took care of our baby. I tried to remain focused, but insecurity and loneliness creeped in and I started instigating petty arguments again. I had now convinced myself that he abandoned me too.

We were in New York and he was in Oklahoma in training. He had given me a ring as a promise of a future together and I was ruining everything. He had only gone as a means of giving us a better advantage and I was adding stress by constantly arguing with him and threatening to leave. We didn't consider the distance and issues his military status would create. Because we weren't married yet, we couldn't go with him. His absence took a toll and I began to see someone on the side. Unbeknownst to me, he began to reach out to his ex-girlfriend from college via letter.

He came home on leave after he completed training and found out I had been talking to someone else. Thereafter, I ran across correspondence with his ex while attempting to retrieve something from his bag. My findings were enough excuse to end the best relationship I'd ever had and I broke off the engagement. Instead of communicating my feelings to him so we could work through it, I decided I needed to leave him before he left me. Our happily ever after never came to fruition.

Honestly, my relationship could have been worked out because our issues weren't that heavy. We were just young with no troubleshooting skills. I had now done to my son what my parents did to me. I unintentionally opened the door for voids to be created in him, single-handedly changing the trajectory of his entire life. I let my pride take away his opportunity to live in a two-parent household and experience a healthy upbringing. I pray one day He can forgive me for that.

I do check in with him from time to time to make sure he doesn't have any voids or residual resentments toward me. I want to be accountable directly to him. He always tells me he doesn't resent me. However, he did recently admit he believed I gave up too easily on my relationship with his dad and felt I could have worked it out. I agree with him. My failure to give my relationship and family a fighting chance will forever be one of my biggest regrets. I hope his father can forgive me as well.

CHAPTER 4

Growing Pains

I missed my son's father and the family we created; I still love him to this day. He was my best friend but my pride wouldn't allow me to tell him. Instead, I kept him at a distance and treated him with hostility. I remained in my miserable home and my grandmother constantly tried to persuade me to work things out with him. I think about it now and feel like she was trying to get me out of there and into a better life but the more she pushed, the further I pushed him away. I refused to admit I was wrong.

My son even plead with me to work it out with his dad. He loved his father so much and just wanted all of us to be together. I'm sure he could also feel my unhappiness. I just looked at him and told him it wasn't going to work out and, he eventually stopped asking. No matter how hard his father tried to restore our relationship, I rejected him. I was still in love with him, but deep down I didn't feel worthy of having someone love me like that. I had never experienced it before him and had never really seen anyone loved like that by their significant other.

We co-parented the best we could. While active duty, he was stationed in Louisiana and supported our child's upbringing with a monthly child-support allotment check. He visited as often as he could (approved leave or not), sometimes driving 24 hours to get to New York and turning around to go back a day or two later. Each time, he returned to his base and I sat lonely, stubborn and craving companionship. Eventually I turned back to seeking love in all the wrong places.

He used to tell me, "You love those hood dudes" and tried for years to get back together with me until he finally gave up, moved on and married someone else. I had the nerve to be jealous. Part of me thought he would be there to catch me when I was ready; what an EGO. One thing I will say, he never turned his back on me and I could go to him if ever I was in need. We have had our issues in some areas but he is the truest friend I have to this day.

"LONELY: Just like you shouldn't go grocery shopping when starving, you should be careful looking for love when lonely. In both cases, you can wind up with unhealthy choices.—Karen Salmansohn

Until recent, my lack of self-love has kept me attached to a man since I was 16 years old with no breaks. I had no room for healing, growth or self-awareness (I am just now getting to truly know who I am as an individual in lieu of someone's wife/girlfriend or mother). My self-worth was dependent upon someone else's validation and it has gotten me hurt repeatedly. When you depend on others to fill you up, you are bound to get disappointed.

I carried every heartbreak, anger, and piece of baggage into the next situation. I was clingy, needy, and emotional and I constantly became "too much" for these men to cohabitate with. It didn't seem unreasonable to me because I was willing to walk through fire with my companion but most were never willing to walk the walk with me. After my break-up with my son's father, I spent the next 20 years gravitating to situations "needing my attention", extending myself beyond my means and never really having it reciprocated. Perhaps, that was one of my issues with my child's father, he wanted me but didn't need me for anything.

I always gave men more than I received and was broken hearted when I got pushed to the side. My abandonment issues always found their way into my relationships and I would literally sit and wait for the other shoe to drop, the day they would leave me too. I found myself buying love, hoping they would stick around. I have even bought things for guys I wasn't in an official relationship with just so they would remain interested. They never did.

When a relationship is built on the wrong things it becomes superficial and when the needs have been met, the interest dissipates. These people knew the trick to keeping me around existed in three little words: I LOVE YOU and to just show me a little attention. It was incredible how the artificial love kept me still but real love made me run. I am very task oriented, I finish what I start and my word is golden and that made me the perfect target for these narcissists. Imagine how different my life would be had I focused that dedication on the right person.

I needed to be attached to someone by any means so, I fell for the "okie doke". I jumped the gun and told men what I was looking for instead of letting them show me who they were and then got disappointed when they didn't meet the mark. I chronically complained, asking for their impossible and holding it against them when they told me a truth I didn't want to hear or see. Too late, I learned to be careful with who I shared my hopes and dreams with because the wrong people could and did use it to their advantage.

My "gift of service" began in 1995 when I started corresponding with a friend during his incarceration. I began to visit him frequently, put money in his account, bought him clothes and food, wrote him and accepted his collect calls. I formed a "relationship" with him and began to revolve my life around being his support system. I did this consistently for about two years and even spent my son's second Christmas on a visit with him while he spent time with his dad, home on military leave.

I was visiting consistently until it became impossible

because my family became homeless again. We were forced to move in with one of my uncle's drug addicted girlfriends until we could get another house. My grandmother, brother, son and I all shared one bedroom in the basement and I continued to be stolen from to include two of the allotment checks my child's father sent home to take care of our son.

Working with limited space, I had to leave our bags of belongings in the hallway. One day, my uncle went through the bags while I was out of the house, found our jewelry and sold it to a local drug dealer. Some of it was returned to my other uncle as the drug dealer was an acquaintance of mine and felt bad.

This was nothing new. Before officially moving out of our home a few months prior, I looked in my dresser draw, opened the box I stored my engagement ring in after my break-up and it was gone! They took my door off the hinges, went into my room and stole it. I felt like someone raped me. I couldn't even pass it along to my son and had the daunting task of telling my child's father it was gone. I no longer had the token of the love I shared with him. They stole from me over and over again.

While in between homes, I continued to talk to my boyfriend on collect calls but the visits were scarce. Out of sight, out of mind, I began seeing a married man (11 years my senior) on the side who was occupying a lot of my time when he could get out of the house. He was stocky in build, strong, handsome, a hard worker, intelligent, extremely funny, street and book smart, and an avid reader. He was a man's man and I felt safe and protected when I was around him (something I had never felt with any other man in my life).

When we met he would pick me up, cradle me in his arms, carry me and call me his little baby. I loved that shit. It wasn't just about sex. Yes, that happened, but many times we were together with opportunity and it didn't happen. We dated--walks in the park, movies, etc., and talked on the phone for hours daily. I was intrigued by him and he was digging me too. I was mature for my age, could keep up with him intellectually and that held his attention for quite some time.

In another space and time, I could have embarked on a relationship with him because above all, we were great friends. Although we clearly crossed the line, he was always honest and never blew smoke up my ass about anything. The timing just wasn't right. As time passed I found myself feeling much too deeply for him. He wasn't free and my conscience was getting the best of me, so I eventually left him alone. To this day, we still maintain a platonic friendship.

I was still walking around angry because my uncle stole my belongings and I didn't get some of it back; irreplaceable

101

things. My other uncle felt I needed to get over it and we got into an argument. It got so heated he told my grandmother he would not assist in paying the mortgage for the house we were due to move into if I was allowed to move with them. His exact words were, "If this Bitch goes, I don't and you need me to help pay the mortgage". I looked at my grandmother and told her, "Don't worry, I'll go". The dispute left me homeless and bouncing from place to place with my two year old. I ended up at my mother's house for a few weeks but we began to clash as I felt she continuously infiltrated my boundaries. For example, I came in the house one day from running an errand and she had a pair of my jeans on without permission. It may not sound like a big deal but for someone accustomed to having their space and belongings violated, it was huge. And, again, she had a tendency to speak condescendingly. I never addressed the jeans thing but I left shortly thereafter.

In spring, 1996, I re-enrolled in school to pursue a Bachelor's degree and started my classes in summer, 1996 while homeless and bouncing around. After experiencing college, continuing on was a no-brainer. I had an insatiable hunger for higher education and success and wasn't going to let any trial and tribulation stop me from bettering myself.

After leaving my mother's house, my son and I moved to the home of a former neighbor and "friend" who had recently suffered the loss of his children's mother and assumed responsibility for the care of his two young daughters. I went into survival mode. My reasoning was he could help me and I could help him, and he lived closer to my school. I began assisting him in the care of his children with additional benefits. This lasted about a month and a half before he became physically abusive because I maintained that he wasn't "my man" (he was also an alcoholic).

When you are in survival mode, it rules out a lot because, you lack resources. You don't care about morality because...you are in survival mode. -Nipsey Hussle

During an argument one day, he hit me in front of my son. My two year old was punching him and screaming, "Get off my mommy!" He pushed me down, my leg buckled under me and I heard my ankle snap. I had a higher tolerance of dealing with abuse than I would ever allow my son to so, I quickly gathered our belongings, grabbed him, limped my ass out of there, went to the hospital for care and moved to a friend's house temporarily. I refused to subject my son to seeing anything like this again and thank God he has no recollection of the event.

The worst part about leaving that situation was the bond I built with his daughters. I loved them very much but had to do what was best for me and mine. My time at my friend's house was also short lived. She made up an excuse about why I could no longer stay there and I left. People are not going to let you crowd their house up for too long.

I eventually moved back into my family home through my grandmother's prompting. The day I returned, my aunt met me at the front door and told me it was my uncle's house and I couldn't come there until I asked his permission to move in. I explained that my grandmother told me to come home and ordered her to get the hell out my way.

She followed me upstairs to the room I was staying in and instructed me not to put my clothes in the dresser as it belonged to my cousin. I told her no problem and continued to live out of plastic bags. All the while, I knew I really didn't have to go through any of that. All I had to do was call my child's father and he would have come to get us at the drop of a dime (not being haughty; just stating a fact). I was so full of pride and ego, insisted on doing things by myself and didn't want to admit I was in over my head. I refused to tell him I was failing miserably. I suffered a lot unnecessarily. He had no idea we were even bouncing around like that.

My son and I were now living in my family home in a small bedroom with a single bed and barely welcome in the environment. It kind of reminded me of my grandmother and me at our relative's home when I was nine years old. I was unhappy and back to being stolen from on a regular basis, but I did my best to stay the course and continued to raise my son and work toward my degree. I also continued to entertain every loser that showed me a little attention.

I was still sporadically in contact with my boyfriend in jail (who had no idea I was homeless). By the end of the second year, the relationship began to falter. I was occupied with school, taking care of my son and working a job in a department store his friend referred me to.

The job went well for a while until extremely stupid and anxious to please my "friends", I hooked someone up. I discounted some merchandise and got caught, resulting in my termination. I was arrested and charged with Petit Larceny and detained for two days at a local jail. I remember being so scared in the interrogation room, looking around, seeing no clear exit. I signed a statement admitting what I had done but, refused to give anyone else's name. They cuffed me, put my leather jacket over my hands and took me to Queens Boulevard to be booked.

I sat there chained to a pole for the rest of the night until they took me downstairs and put me in a cell. I sat on the floor looking at my son's pictures (the C.O. let me take them with me) thinking how disappointed he would be to know his mother broke the law as I always drilled right from wrong into his three year old head.

Inmates came around giving out sandwiches with green bologna and a carton of milk and I just gave it away. I was eventually moved to a large bullpen with a bunch of women while I waited to see the judge. That was my first experience in seeing someone withdraw off heroin. The lady was shivering and kept asking the C.O. if she had something sweet for her to eat. Naturally, they couldn't give her anything. I just told her not to worry, it would be okay.

The next challenge was for me to call my grandmother. I called home earlier while I was in the interrogation room at the store because she had my son. She picked up the phone and I immediately asked her to put my father on the phone. When he answered I told him what happened and he promised not to tell my grandmother until I could tell her myself. She questioned him about my whereabouts all night and he kept his word.

The next day, I called home and told her where I was. She started crying, "Why you? Anybody else but you". I was so ashamed, I just cried with her and apologized profusely. My aunt got on the phone yelling and telling me how stupid I was. I couldn't argue because she was right.

I sat in Central Booking the entire weekend, talked to a

public defender and finally went in front of the judge on Monday night. My aunt and a family friend came to court for support and I was released on my own recognizance. At first I walked far ahead of my aunt because I honestly thought she was going to fuck me up. When she saw the shame in my face she put her hand on my shoulder from behind. I threw myself in her arms and started crying. She assured me everything was going to be okay.

I went back and forth to court for a few months and was eventually sentenced to "Adjournment in Contemplation of a Dismissal" as long as I completed seven days of community service and a "Stop-Lift" program. I was in college, majoring in Criminal Justice and now I had a record. I completed my obligation immediately and by the grace of God my record was wiped clean. It was one of the dumbest things I've ever done and I've never been in trouble since. I was ashamed, extremely remorseful and grateful for a second chance.

I was scared to tell my boyfriend because, his friend had gotten me the job, so I avoided visiting him. I eventually told him and he exploded. Released soon thereafter, we gave the relationship a try for a short period of time but he left me for a girl he was seeing on the side. Honestly, I knew it wasn't going to work. He had just regained his freedom and I had a small child I had to take care of, so that hindered my availability. (It was never my expectation for any man to take on a fatherly role toward my son). He called me on the phone to break it off with me, I agreed and moved on. We were only meant to be friends and that's what we are today, friends with a mutual respect for one another.

College was again a great addition to my life as it exposed me to encouraging and driven people. I was attending St. John's University. While there, I pledged Zeta Phi Beta Sorority, Inc. and was surrounded by strong, ambitious women who became pillars of support in my life. They took a liking to my son and I formed a few great friendships I still maintain to this day.

College kept me out of my house. It presented an environment where I could soar; I even took my son to class with me sometimes. When I was there, I felt like a different person with unlimited possibilities. When I was home I was reminded of my limitations so, I stayed out of the house as long as I could. I attended school from 8 am to 12 noon and worked for my welfare benefits at a local hospital from 1 pm to 5 pm.

In 1998, right before graduation, tragedy struck my family. The attic of my house caught fire due to an over-utilized extension cord and my 10 year old sister was burned over 75 percent of her body.

My bedroom sat directly below the area involved and I could hear my siblings and cousins running down the steps. Not knowing how large or severe the fire was, I followed my first instinct to get water. While filling up a pot, I heard my sister screaming from the attic. I ran back upstairs with the water and my cousin and I worked together to pull her out of the fire.

I saw the effects of her burns first-hand before she was rendered treatment. I can still see the gray smoke in the attic and the exposed bones in the heels of her feet in my psyche. Her red flannel nightgown was hanging off her body and her feet were so badly burned she dropped to her knees after I walked her to my grandmother, who was in the bathroom running water in the tub and wetting sheets.

My sister was rushed to a hospital burn unit in the city where she fought for her life and died a month later. I've lived with guilt for years, wondering if I could have done more to avoid her death and had that further enhanced when my aunt asked me "why I didn't run up the steps faster". She told me if it were my son, I would have moved quicker. I wondered why she would say something like that to me when anyone that truly knows me knows I would sacrifice myself before I would see anyone I love harmed. I guess grief does that sometimes and I don't hold it against her, I just did self-inventory to be sure I did all I could.

We were relocated to a temporary home for a few months and forced to move back to the same house once it was repaired. My family was constantly reminded of our loss. My trauma over the incident was so bad I never set foot in that attic again and would flip out if I saw my son even go near it. He had strict instructions to never go in the attic.

S.T.G.-9/10/1987-2/1/1998-Forever in my Heart

A few months after the fire, my son's father returned home from deployment in Bosnia and came to see us. He gained knowledge of my sister's death while deployed but was unable to attend the funeral (He was very close to her and saddened by the loss as well). We tried briefly to rekindle our relationship but it never happened.

Eventually, I began dating a guy I had known for years. I ran into him in the train station, he rapped to me, gave me a copy of one of his mix tapes, invited me on an Atlantic City trip he was hosting and we began seeing each other. He was a bit more "boisterous" than I liked but, I rolled with it. Eventually he became jealous, possessive, and verbally abusive.

He paid a lot of attention to me at first, called daily, took me out, bought me things and there was nothing I couldn't ask him for but it was impossible to go anywhere with him. If we went out to dinner I would often sit with my head down in a menu because he would cause a scene if he believed someone was looking at me. He would often accuse me of commanding extra attention.

I disregarded all the red flags and eventually moved in with him at his mother's home. She was kind to me but he was disrespectful, mean, would kick me out every other week and was emotionally abusive. He would call me fat and threaten to leave me if I didn't lose weight and have a baby and I tolerated it because, living with him in a "quieter" environment got me away from the dysfunction in my family home. At least I wasn't being stolen from anymore right?

I didn't like how he interacted with my son and I wasn't going to have him abusing him, so I left him in my grandmother's care during the week so I could work and he could travel to school with my siblings and cousins and I was with him on the weekends.

One night, during one of his tirades, he kicked me out. He even called my father who was at the peak of his addiction and told him to come get me before he hit me.

To this day, I don't know what triggered the outburst. My father dropped what he was doing, hopped on a bike and came to get me out of there. I hold on to times like that when I recall the times my father fell short. That day, he stepped up and I appreciated that.

His mother told me I needed to leave him, that one day, I would get a "belly full" and I would leave. Nobody knows a person better than their mother. I always built good rapports with a majority of these guy's mothers. They saw the good in me, I just didn't think I deserved better. I eventually went back and remained in this relationship for another year before he began to cheat on me with a girl at work, moved out of state with her and left me living in his mother's house.

I worked daily and continued to live there for about a month before his mother told me I had to move out; thank God she did or else I would have sat there longer feeling sorry for myself. I worked nights at a hospital so I bounced back and forth between my grandmother's house and a friend's house for a few months to sleep and bathe before saving up enough money to get my first apartment.

My best friend's parents were gracious enough to allow me to rent an apartment in their home. They are beautiful people and like second parents to me and I am forever grateful to them for being instrumental in me getting on my feet.

Lacking progressive direction, I moved on to the next live wire. He was an incarcerated guy three years younger than me. I didn't know him from the street, I saw a picture and asked someone to introduce me to him. Of course he jumped at the chance to correspond, why wouldn't he? I was an opportunity. I began to visit him and formed a new "relationship". This guy had been a lifetime criminal, in and out of jail from the age of 18.

He was mean, disrespectful and not appealing to me at all. But, I saw other people on the side and stayed around because he "needed" me. I was visiting, sending him packages, taking his collect calls and when he got released, I moved him into my new apartment. BIG MISTAKE!

He was of no real help to me and may have given me money toward the household one or two times; I never pushed the issue. I never held men at any real standard and walked around under the guise that I didn't need a man to provide for me. The women in my life *appeared* to have never asked men for anything either, they just made it happen so I followed the same routine.

This guy cheated on me, was in and out of jail and was physically abusive. I was fighting all the time because I was not going to let him beat me down. My family had no confirmation of this but they speculated. I recall a time I had a bruise the size of a grapefruit on my leg from fighting him. I was at my grandmother's house spending time with my son and my uncle spotted it. He put his fist next to the bruise to compare and just looked at me. I didn't say a word. My other uncle took me to the hospital another time, unaware that I had even been assaulted by this guy. I just told him I didn't feel good and needed to go to the hospital.

To add insult to injury, this dude was another factor that I allowed to keep me away from my son because I wasn't going to have him seeing someone beat on his mother. Accordingly, he remained with my grandmother during the week and came to me on the weekends.

Bear in mind, I took care of my son financially, never missed major milestones and was very active in his life. I took him to every first day of school (all the way into college), was present for award ceremonies and school trips if I could get off of work. I did everything to ensure he didn't miss me but for four years, my baby didn't live with me full time because I was walking in circles, trying to find myself and running from my pain.

I felt I was protecting him and in some ways that's valid, but I was also denying him full-time access to his mother. He always tells me I did a good job as his mom but I know he would have appreciated being with me every day and not just on the weekends in that aspect of his life. I'm sorry Torey.

One thing I never did was lie to him. In fact, I was

brutally honest and believe it contributed to his thick skin and realistic views on life. Once again, you have to tell children the truth or eventually they won't respect you. Believe me, they can handle it. I knew he was safe with my grandmother but I wasn't safe in her home because I was subject to violation on a daily basis; ripped off on a regular basis.

I remained largely protective of my son but didn't hold myself in the same esteem. I rationalized that each abusive situation I entered was far less severe than anything I would go through had I remained in my family home. I looked at those relationships as something I just needed to get through, a direct reflection of my upbringing.

My boyfriend was locked up often so, I had plenty of breaks. During one of his incarcerations, he asked me during a visit if I had put money into his account. When I told him I didn't have it he said, "I should spit in your face". Livid, I kicked a table into his leg, walked off the visit and never went back. But, I continued to uphold my commitment to this lie of a relationship. I put money on his books and took his calls and he continued to be cold, mean, obnoxious, and barely speak a kind word to me. I connected to him because I saw a commonality in our backgrounds.

We had both lost parents to addiction and were raised by

our grandmothers. I looked at him and saw all the things I felt: fear, brokenness, defensiveness and hurt, and I wanted to save him. I wanted to be there for him, but I now realize people like that will destroy you before you ever heal them. He was released again and the abuse continued.

The physical abuse got so bad I started avoiding my family because I was bruised up. I never involved them in any of my issues. I got myself into the mess, I would get myself out. Our family was dysfunctional but we loved each other. Also, I had a brother who was not to be played with; especially when it came to me. I wasn't going to risk him being in trouble for my bad choices so I lied to him about what was going on.

The last straw came with finding a firearm in a shoe box in my house. Thank God my son never came in contact with it. Or, my siblings and cousins for that matter because they frequented my home as well. I also caught him red-handed with a girl in his car and had a fist fight later that day that resulted in him punching me and swelling my face up. I later received news that he had the same girl pregnant. She was calling my phone harassing me and I told her she could have him, I was finally done.

Instead of putting him out of my house, I decided to leave. It seemed easier than trying to get him out. I didn't tell my landlord what I was going through because I was ashamed (I'm sure they knew though). I notified them of my impending departure, arranged to live out my security deposit and made a few phone calls to my mother who was now living in Baltimore. I told her I was interested in relocating and asked if I could stay on her couch until I could figure it out, she said yes.

After discussing the relocation with my son's father, he agreed. I asked my aunt to keep my son for a year so he could finish his last year in elementary school and I could put things in place for us, she agreed. All bases were covered and I booked my ticket to Baltimore.

I couldn't think of one reason to remain in New York. My backbone (my grandmother) had passed away almost two years prior and I simply did not have anyone to support me or love me unconditionally the way she did. A lifetime of stress eventually took a toll on her. A heavy smoker, she died at the age of 67 from pancreatic cancer. Our family divided even more and none of us knew what we were going to do without her.

The cancer ran rampant through her body and took her fairly quickly. My aunt and I spent the last weekend of her life in the hospital and unfortunately had to witness her body prepare to expire. We held a bucket under her mouth as she vomited blood and comforted her through embarrassment when it came through her anus as well. The day she died, I went home to shower and change clothes with plans to return to the hospital for another night. When I got there, she had already passed on. I was so hysterical I had to be placed on oxygen. Eventually, I calmed myself down, returned to her room and climbed in the bed with her body where I began to sing the same song she used to sing to me as a child. Her death was another hard lesson in growth, I didn't have her to fall back on anymore. I will always feel her absence in the physical but, I certainly feel her presence in the spiritual.

I packed a duffel bag with interview clothes and a few pair of jeans and sneakers, hopped on Amtrak and moved out of New York. No apartment or job waiting for me in the new place but anything would be better than the hell I was going through. I took Amtrak and once I purchased a car drove back and forth to New York monthly to visit my son.

CHAPTER 5

Relocation... I'm Really Running from My Problems

I didn't know what I was walking into when I moved to Baltimore. I moved to a sketchy neighborhood to stay with my mother until I could figure it out. My child's father, on military duty in Maryland at the time, picked me up from the train station, took me to my destination, and made sure I settled in safely before he returned to his life. I sat for the first few days crying my eyes out, hurt over what I had just left and of course feeling homesick because this was definitely not New York. I missed my son but I was doing it for us and had to make it work so we could be together full-time again. I arrived on a Friday, got up the next Monday and hit the pavement.

I made my way to the downtown business sector and passed out as many resumes as I could. My luck began to brighten when I stopped into a restaurant, applied for a job as a waitress and was hired on the spot. I had a job by the end of the first week and would do that to make money until I could secure an administrative job.

The restaurant mostly employed ex-offenders and I ended up meeting and latching on to one of them. He seemed like a nice enough guy and paid me a lot of attention. He was occupying my time and keeping my mind off what I had left behind. He had also just been released from serving a lengthy sentence, was still living in a halfway house and was a recovering heroin addict who eventually turned to alcohol. I spent a lot of time with him and also became close with his sister.

My tenure at my mother's house lasted about a month and a half as the environment didn't meet my needs and we couldn't get along. I didn't care for the area and was not going to bring my son there to live. Her approach was dictatorial and I could not mentally receive suggestion from her. I wanted her to butt out of my life. She was however, right about the mistake I was making in dealing with this guy.

He ended up being my "saving grace" after an argument and physical altercation with my mother and a quick exit from her house with nowhere to go. I couldn't go back to New York and let my family know I'd failed so I was searching for other options. Now living with his parents, I went home with him that night and slept outside on his porch as they didn't allow girls to sleep over. Thank God it was summertime.

The next day, he explained my situation and asked them to take me in and they agreed (grateful). I paid them $25 a week in rent and worked around the clock to save up to move. Thank God my aunt was holding my son down for me and I had comfort in knowing he was safe. There was no way I would have let him go through that with me, I would have gone back to New York.

I worked a temp job at a hospital by day and waitressed at night. My day started at 7:30 a.m. and ended at 2:00 a.m. the next day. I saved up enough for a down payment on an apartment in two months and the guy helped me find a place in a better part of town because I was still learning my way around the city.

Not wanting to live with another man, I went against my better judgment and allowed him to move in because I felt I owed him for helping me out. I felt trapped because my environment changed but my situation really didn't. I was making the same mistakes over and over again.

Eight months later my son and sister moved down to live with me and I finally had him back with me full-time. I immediately enrolled him in private school. Working both a full and part time job, I was slowly but surely getting my life on track.

My sister was also a great help to me as she looked out for him and made sure he got home from school while I worked. Naturally, the relationship with the guy was crashing and burning. He began cheating on me and making excuses about how much rent he couldn't afford to contribute. He eventually moved out but lingered here and there.

I wasn't getting it right in my personal relationships but I remained motivated in my career and education. I decided to enroll in a program to work toward a Master's degree, at first opting to enter an interdisciplinary studies program and eventually settling into a major in Human Resource Development.

I was preparing to start my first semester in about a week and things were looking up until all the stress I endured over the years finally came to a head in the form of a perforated ulcer. I hadn't been feeling good for months and ignored the signs. I experienced frequent headaches, bloating, fatigue and muscle spasms in my left arm.

My aunt was visiting for the weekend to attend a Bat-Mitzvah with me. She made a nice dinner and we were all sitting around watching television when I began having excruciating pain in my left arm. I asked her to rub my arm but couldn't get any relief. The pain became so intense I began to scream and cry. Sweating profusely, I crawled to the kitchen floor and sat there on all fours trying to cool my body temperature down.

My son sat beside me with a horrified look on his face while I assured him I was okay. My aunt called an ambulance and I was rushed to a local hospital. My sister sat with me all night until they could figure out what was wrong and after performing various tests, they finally found the issue and began to prep me for emergency exploratory surgery.

I walked around with a hole in my stomach lining for months until I became septic and fell ill. The doctor said if I had waited any longer to come in, I would have died. Some of my family came running to my side from out of state (my grandfather, father, brother's mother, aunt and uncle) and my son's father checked in via telephone. I was hospitalized for five days and had a tube down my nose for two days to clean out excess bacteria. The surgery left me with 37 staples down the middle of my stomach and on disability for six weeks.

My aunt brought my son to the hospital the day after surgery and I will never forget the expression on his face. He saw that tube down my nose and burst into tears; he was just 11 years old. He had never seen me in such a vulnerable position before. My little man did all he could to help me while I was on disability. He carried grocery bags and put them away, held my hand while I walked to and from the car and made sure I didn't do anything too strenuous.

My supervisor, also my friend ensured all my affairs at work were in order, arranged it so my sister could cover my desk until I returned to work and stuck close to me as a pillar of support, even to the point of washing me up when I couldn't do it for myself. I am forever grateful to her.

Getting sick was a pivotal moment in my life because it helped me release old emotions. For years I suppressed and walked in anger with a very hard exterior. Having to have emergency surgery was a shock. I had no time to prepare myself mentally and it scared the hell out of me. The aftermath left me so weak that a simple walk to the bathroom put me to sleep and I developed a terrible case of acid reflux. My brother's mother stayed at my house for the first week to take care of me and I really appreciated that because I could barely walk and definitely could not drive.

For quite some time, I walked around ashamed of the scar and also found my nerves to be frazzled. I would hold my hands in front of me and they would just shake. Holding things in and acting like I didn't care provided a protective barrier; it kept me defensive and hard as a brick wall. After the surgery, I couldn't hold my emotions any more. I had crying fits, lashed out and began to bluntly say how I felt about everything. It was a good thing because I was finally ridding myself of the monkey on my back. It was bad because my delivery was not always good. Sometimes, my delivery is *still* not good.

My stomach perforated and my defenses crumbled. I was "showing my hand" and revealing that things bothered and hurt me. It took me a long time to realize it was beneficial to get it out and eventually I began to look at my scar in a positive light. It saved my life in more ways than one.

I was still eager to pursue my Master's degree so, I dropped two of my four classes and started graduate school for the semester. I was walking across campus and climbing steps to get to class with staples in my stomach but I was determined to stay on track.

To add insult to injury, while out on disability, I received notice from my complex that I had to vacate for renovations. That left me tasked with finding a new place to live in a short period of time. I made it happen and continued to recover.

The guy had moved out but seized the opportunity to run to my side during distress while continuing to covertly add stress. I slowly distanced myself and went back to work a few weeks later. When I returned, I started to connect with one of the patients from my second job in a dialysis unit.

I had known him for a little while and he was recently separated from his wife. In the past, he would converse with me every time he came to the unit for treatment. We started speaking on the phone and spending a little time together. He was charming, could cook, and was flashy

125

with his money (which turned out to be a product of his monthly disability check). I fell for it and began to see him regularly.

The other guy was still trying to come around but, I wasn't interested. My rejection caused him to pursue me more aggressively and one day while ignoring his attempt to contact me, he broke into my apartment, kicked my bedroom door in, and upon seeing my new friend (who was visiting at the time) struck me in the face several times. He did this two months after I had major surgery on my stomach so I steadied my stance and blocked my face instead of fighting him back. The new guy just sat there and watched. I threatened to call the police so he left, but continued to harass me intermittently over the next year.

He was calling my job daily and having other people do it as well, telling me to move back to New York or he would have someone hurt my son, stabbed my tires flat, keyed my brand new car on all sides, broke my windshield wiper down to the arm and did all he could to cause me to fall ill again. The police would not allow me to press charges because I could never prove it so, I continued to live my life and eventually, he stopped. I also continued to pursue a relationship with the new guy.

We were seeing each other for about 4 months and he began having housing issues. Yup, you guessed it! Nova saves the day...I let him move in. That's when I started to see the other side. He was a heavy marijuana smoker and drinker, had major medical issues, stole money from me a few times, totaled my brand new car, was manipulative, a major embellisher and a habitual liar.

I lost interest after about six months but I allowed him to remain in my home for years, even after the official break-up because I didn't want to be the cause of him being homeless. He paid his rent on time and I was grateful for the financial assistance. Also, preferring a monogamous situation, I had live in sex if I wanted it, until I stopped wanting that too. My family and friends thought I was nuts. They were right.

After I moved to Baltimore, a few more family members followed over the years. My father came to live with me first and I eventually took on the care of my youngest sister when she was 17. She remained with me through her completion of high school. I spent a number of years catering to them and my ex-boyfriend's needs, with one of my sisters and the ex-boyfriend being the only ones providing any financial assistance. *After constant disagreement with our father, my sister moved out (she did what was best for her; I don't blame her) and that put further financial strain on me.*

At one point, I had two siblings, my father, and my ex-boyfriend living in my two bedroom apartment. This required my son to share his space. He finally had his own bedroom and now he had to share but he never complained. My father was my largest responsibility as he wouldn't maintain employment and continued with his attitude of entitlement. I felt responsible for his well-being.

I thought if I kept him close and made him feel cared for and protected, he wouldn't start getting high again. It was my insurance that he would stay out of trouble. I've spent a great deal of his sobriety afraid that he would relapse. I now realize I could hold him as close as I wanted but maintaining sobriety was up to him. I charged up my credit cards to clothe and feed him and often put his needs before my own. Eventually, he met someone and moved in with her.

To be transparent, I had mixed emotions when he moved out my house. It began with visiting her and soon thereafter, he didn't return. He didn't have a conversation with me to let me know he would be moving out and in with his girlfriend, he just left. I felt used for my assistance and thrown away when the next best thing came along. I walked around angry at him for a while but eventually realized it was a good thing. He got married and is relatively on a productive and independent path. I'm proud of him.

The ex-boyfriend continued to linger with no intention of vacating and it took something very adverse to cause me to finally put him out of my house. His presence wasn't inconvenient for me all those years because I functioned in life disregarding him. I completely moved on with my life and would walk past him like he wasn't there. I am very good at blocking things out when they become too much or irrelevant. He contributed to the rent so I treated him like a tenant--strictly platonic.

Moving forward, he began to drink again and exhibit erratic behavior and I began to discover the items in my bedroom were out of place. One day, I caught him walking into my room when he thought I wasn't home. The last straw, one night at about 2 a.m., I kept hearing noises from the staircase leading to my room. I got up, turned on the light and he was sitting at the top of the steps. I kicked him so hard in his back he almost fell down the steps. That night, I confronted him and gave 30 days to vacate my home. He left with a lot of urging.

CHAPTER 6

The One

This relationship was supposed to be my forever. From the naked eye it looked doomed from the beginning and people tried to warn me but I didn't want to hear it. For the first time in over 20 years, I was in love. There wasn't anything anyone could tell me about him-THIS was going to work.

I had known him since I was 15/16. We had a brief thing, nothing serious and life took us in different directions. I walked my journey and he got lost in the streets eventually finding himself incarcerated. Fast forward 17 years and we were reconnected through his friend while he was in prison.

It started off as two old friends corresponding. I was adamant about keeping it platonic and maintained that for about a year. Old habits die hard though and I fell into my previous routine, sending money, written correspondence, telephone calls and visitation. I traveled to several states to see him as he was transferred to six different places in seven years.

Something was "different" about him from all the others. I could talk to him about any subject. He was a great conversationalist and spiritually sound, almost devout.

We read books together and I learned from him. I was being mentally fed and it was refreshing. The four guys before him couldn't keep my interest for long; they had no substance and I was never mentally stimulated. I hadn't experienced a connection like this since my child's father.

I was so comfortable talking to him I quickly began to divulge my deepest inner thoughts and feelings. I told him everything about myself, my hurt, fears and triumphs. I left no stone unturned and was completely vulnerable. I wanted him to know me and where I had been because I knew I was coming to the table with a lot of unresolved baggage. I didn't want to misrepresent myself, but most of all, if he was going to love me, I wanted him to love the entire me.

By doing this, I didn't realize I was giving him ammunition. He listened intently and also told me a lot about his personal and familial history. He told me just enough for me to empathize and in some ways relate. We bonded and he became my best friend and confidante.

I loved him so much and for a long time felt safe with him. I used to hug him, hold my face to his and smell his skin just so I could take him in. I hung on his every word. He made me happy and everyone could see it. I looked forward to every opportunity to be with him. For years he was kind, doting, complimentary, and seemed to care about my well-being.

I felt so comfortable sharing and trusted him so much I began to disregard red flags and didn't realize when he started spitting my words back at me. Certain aspects of my life became his life, some of my fears became his fears.

In the midst of sharing his past he would reveal inflammatory things about prior relationships. I didn't question it because he seemed to take just enough responsibility for his negative actions to satisfy my belief that he was owning up to his short comings. His stories had me angry at people I didn't even know and when I voiced disdain for what they had "done to him", he questioned why I was bothered by it. He played a serious mind game and I was so caught up I didn't even realize he was doing it.

He would very subtly tell me how much the prior women doted on him and made great sacrifices to be with him. It made me feel like I was in competition with them and I began trying to "one-up". That's exactly where he wanted me to be because it guaranteed I too would go to great lengths to ensure he was good.

He never asked me to do anything that would compromise my freedom or integrity and I would never have allowed that anyway, but before long, he had me spinning like a top. I would send him my last $20 if he said he needed it.

He even reached out to my son, aunt and sister via letter

to reassure them I was in good hands and developed what appeared to be a great bond with one of my sisters. The other sister and one of my uncles kept their distance and remained skeptical. My other immediate family members, though apprehensive, supported my relationship and welcomed him with open arms. They too began to provide him with support, some through correspondence, and others through visits. They saw how happy I was so they accepted it. My aunt, dead set against it in the beginning, even started to lighten up and went to visit him.

The relationship progressed steadily with him mentioning marriage a few times. I fell more and more in love and by the third year mark, we got married. Most people say it's never ideal to marry someone in prison and I was going to be there for him whether we got married or not, but it felt good to have someone else that loved me enough to want to marry me. I loved him that much too and felt safe with him so, I accepted the proposal. I felt like this was my second chance at happily ever after. My sister and his friend stood as witnesses, it was a great day and I felt at peace with my decision. My sisters even threw me a bridal shower.

We moved forward with life and I continued to support him 100%. My life revolved around him and I advocated for every cause outside the norm concerning him and his well-being. I ran to his beck and call, made sure he had everything he needed, traveled far distances to see him and made myself available by any means.

We faced major hurdles for the future as he would be deported upon his release but I didn't care. I would move there with him and that was the plan. I didn't care what I had to sacrifice as long as we could be together.

Once again, I saw red flags throughout the entire relationship but I ignored it. He could be manipulative, was irresponsible with money, told inconsistent stories and I caught him in a few lies. I would address the behavior and he would take responsibility enough to appease me, promise to work on it and I would shut up.

Still, I felt an insecure feeling inside that I fought off constantly but eventually started asking a myriad of questions. I believe it was my spirit talking to me but I focused on what was good, remained loyal and consistent and fought for our marriage.

Things began to go awry about a year before his release. He became snappy and blamed it on anxiety over his impending release. His contact with me began to wane but my presence and support never did. As the release date drew near, I continued to prepare and he began to downsize his property and send things home.

These things included a calculated/strategic box of belongings. When I received the box, it was damaged and falling apart. In the process of transferring the stuff to another box, I found what I believe was planted evidence of infidelity. There were recent letters, pictures and cards from old flings (nobody is dumb enough to leave items like that in a box and send it home to their wife).

I waited for him to call and hit the roof. He began to gaslight me, turning it around on me asking why I went through the box. I was incredulous, was I really not supposed to open the box? He was insistent that none of it meant anything but I was destroyed inside. I felt like a fool and my world came crashing down. Every bit of trust I had in him was gone. My worst nightmare had come true.

I went through the typical rants, yelling that I wanted a divorce, telling him not to speak to me anymore, called out of work because I didn't want to get out of bed etc., but he worked on me and before long, I was back in line. I continued to prepare for the life we (I) had been looking forward to for years and tried to keep my insecurities at bay.

He was released to his birth country and I wasn't far behind. I flew in and we took care of everything we needed in order to get him acclimated and prepare for my relocation to the country. Over the weeks I was there, things were okay but, I had to return to the United States. We were back to phone calls and visits. The difference was, he was free this time. Free to explore, meet new people and he began to change even more. My insecurity and jealousy was heightened and I was calling as often as I could because when I didn't speak to him, my mind was racing, wondering what else he might be doing to betray me.

As time went on, he called me less and less and if I called, I was accused of smothering him. If I complained or questioned, I was crazy. He began to freeze me out and eventually weeks would pass by before I heard from him; most often when he needed something. I held true to my vows and continued to support. The more tumultuous things got, the deeper I dug my heels in and stood strong.

I wanted him to know I had his back, tried to be the best wife I could but, I was heartbroken and so insecure. I didn't even recognize him anymore. He became mean and cold and I was accumulating more and more evidence of infidelity. I was due to move to the country with him in a few months, lining up job interviews and one day, he told me not to come.

The month I was supposed to move there, he sent me visual evidence of adultery and cut off complete contact with me for a year. I plunged into the deepest bowels of depression and lost an exorbitant amount of weight. I continued to work and take care of my responsibilities but, each day, I came home, made my room completely dark and went straight to bed. On the weekends, I didn't bother to get out of bed at all. I slept all the time because I didn't want to think about or feel the pain. My sister walked that dark road with me, held me in her arms and wiped my tears many days.

My family was asking questions but, I was withdrawn and quiet so they left me alone. I told myself, "Don't open up. All they are going to say is I told you so". My heart was so sick when we separated. I couldn't wrap my mind around it (part of me still can't but, I know it happened for a good reason).

I felt used, confused, tired, humiliated and abandoned once again. I had a few trusted people I chose to talk to because I couldn't make sense of it. I needed someone to tell me why he did this because I couldn't get the answers from him. I wore my sister's ear out hoping she could help me figure out something I knew she couldn't. It turned out I was never able to get any relief so I stopped talking and turned inward and upward.

My marriage had broken up and I felt like a failure. I couldn't figure out what I had done wrong. I isolated and watched "WhatsApp" and his Facebook page obsessively but I stood strong in my convictions and refused any attempt to make contact with him. I trudged through my pain over the next year and on my next birthday he made contact. It was all I had longed for and about all he had done over the last year. I suffered, cried and was still angry but I longed for him at the same time. I quickly allowed him back into my space. I was holding on to who I remembered.

I tried everything to save my marriage and find forgiveness. I was willing to put the past behind me and try to work it out but he only made contact according to his convenience. I learned the more I gave emotionally and financially, the more he (and others in my lifetime) took without ever reciprocating.

I began to take a look at my life as a whole and realize how many narcissistic personalities I had been dealing with over the last 15-20 years, in my intimate relationships and over my lifetime within my family. I was disgusted and felt duped.

Before long, I began to open my eyes and realize he re-established contact because he was using me as a resource and for self-gratification as well. I began creating boundaries, saying no and taking my power back. I also seized the opportunity to ask some vital questions so I could achieve some semblance of closure and he did give me a few answers. He eventually cut off contact again because all the questions were too much "pressure".

The contact restored again after a few months but continued to be sporadic and eventually, I found out he had someone pregnant. My initial reaction to the news was numbness. I was so used to being hurt I couldn't even

THE SLEEPER HAS AWAKENED

cry at first. I didn't confront him and I even continued to respond if he contacted me. Even through all the betrayal and hurt, I still craved his attention, even if it was miniscule.

My head was spinning. I knew his actions were unacceptable but I was still trying to place myself in his shoes and convinced myself I was letting him find his way while I was finding mine. It seemed like nothing was a deal breaker. I was selective with my words and afraid to express my feelings regarding how he treated me because I didn't want him to stop speaking to me altogether. I evaluated his background over and over again because I knew where he had been. I rationalized that he may have removed himself from my life to avoid hurting me further. I still tried to give him the benefit of the doubt because once again, I knew his story. I had compassion for him.

I reminded myself he was incarcerated at a young age, was gone for a long time and forced to suppress his emotions for survival's sake. I told myself, "He doesn't really know how to love". "What he wanted and what he was capable of doing were two very different things". "Perhaps he just didn't have it in him to be what he signed up to be". Never once did I feel hate, just disappointment and hurt. I tried to convince myself I hated him to cope, but I didn't.

I have put myself through a mental rollercoaster trying to

process the whole thing and realize I have been guilty of hearing what I wanted to hear instead of reading between the lines. Sometimes, people don't shoot straight but their actions tell you everything you need to know.

Regardless, healing and changing him is not my responsibility. I pray for his healing and hope he wants that for himself as well. Sometimes, you have to love people from a distance and I continue to do that. Love is not always enough to sustain a marriage. You need mutual dedication, communication, brutal honesty, forgiveness and the desire to fight it out together. If these components are missing, it will be hard to keep it together. And the effort definitely can't be one-sided.

I fight every day to overcome because he was and still is a MAJOR part of my heart, but I'm focused on my own healing and putting myself first (after God). I'm taking my life back from this situation and all the other offenses that have occurred in my life. Somehow, I believe my heart was broken that deeply to wake me up. Otherwise, the cycle would have never been broken. I would have ridden that wave as long as I could. Believe me, I never would have left him on my own because I loved him that much and took my vows very seriously.

I lost someone I loved more than I loved myself and that was the issue. I didn't love myself completely and the little bit I did have, I loved him more. I'm still not at 100%

self-love but, I'm getting there. I couldn't recover from the devastation of the heartbreak because I poured everything into him. My cup was so empty I couldn't replenish myself enough to rise above. I had been in that predicament so many times before.

The bottom line is, I took a man that had no knowledge of self, no direction and no peace and tried to build a life with him. I knew there were deficiencies but I loved him anyway. I was willing to meet him in the middle and grow with him but he wasn't there yet. I was further along than he was and I still had growing to do.

Although a very sensitive and private matter, it was necessary for me to divulge this piece of my life, but don't misunderstand. I'm not here to slander or play the blame game, just take responsibility for my mistakes, forgive him for his and be grateful for the goodness and lessons in the union I shared with him because we did have a lot of good times.

He's a good guy, just a product of circumstance and I'll always love and pray for him. Most of all, I don't regret the decision to be with him or marry him because I know the pieces of him beyond the naked eye. I also loved him sincerely and had the very best intentions going in. Why should I regret following my heart? I may not like how things went down but, I understand what motivated him to handle things the way he did. I look at my side and try to see his side as well, as I have done with so many others.

One day I will be able to thank him and all the others that hurt me. Those experiences propelled me to where I am today, kicking and screaming, and have been influential in my ongoing evolution. It forced me to truly get to know myself because I really didn't know who I was aside from being a support system for others.

The heartbreak shook me to my core but it really wasn't about hurting me, it was to help me. It was about opening my eyes, forcing me to take a look at myself and pinning me so far in a corner I would have no choice but to make some changes. Now that I'm clearer and wiser, I refuse to go down the beaten path ever again and am more open minded to things outside my comfort zone because I've been sitting in a box my whole life.

I'm discovering what I want and realizing how much I've settled just to survive and feel valid. I am learning to stop crucifying myself every time I make a mistake and not to allow anyone else to crucify me either. I'm going through this process slowly, on my own terms and I won't allow anyone to rush me. Believe me, people have certainly tried. I'll get there...

CHAPTER 7

The Crash

I made so many people, including my husband, responsible for my happiness. I made him responsible for picking up pieces he didn't break and responsible for my well-being when he too was broken. I was looking to him for what I wanted from my parents, my friends and my partner. He had one job and I wanted him to perform all three. I owe him an apology for that.

I didn't see the error in my choices because I was only asking for what I had set forth to do for him. We were both wrong. I took on a job that wasn't mine and he made me promises he knew he couldn't keep. Intentions don't always match capabilities.

"You disrespect yourself every time you say yes when you want to say no. You call it loyalty/love/friendship. Really, you're just hoping someone will see how amazing you are and choose you. It shouldn't work that way. Choose yourself. That's how you teach them, by choosing you". – Unknown

That heartbreak brought much more to the surface, on top of the revelation I received from my stomach episode. I attended counseling for a while but, when I started feeling better, I let it lapse and began to suppress again. I stopped dealing with the left over baggage and put a Band-Aid on the wounds by occupying the space with men, work and school. Trauma is like addiction, it's never cured. That short tenure in therapy was not going to heal all those years of suffering. Therapy needed to be ongoing and I'm working my way back to it.

I battled depression for three years after my break-up and quite often, I still cry over the heartbreak and the rejection. For a while, the depth of my depression caused me to become "martyr-like", just sitting in agony, defense and combativeness. When out of seclusion, I was provoked by the smallest slight. My personal and business worlds began to merge, something I had never allowed before. Every time someone did something that remotely reminded me of past experiences, I would revert back and fly off the handle, sometimes to the point of becoming physical.

I struggle with socializing more than ever because I'm extremely limited in who I trust. Still, I don't believe everyone is against me, I'm aware that I have work to do too. I just find it hard to cope with the deja-vu. I have to remind myself that people have their shit just like I do and their own inabilities to cope, that sometimes, they deflect.

I also realize some people are just not interested in listening or supporting you through your pain, the energy might be too heavy. Empathy is difficult when a person can't relate. Unintentionally they become insensitive, claiming what they would never allow to happen in their lives. I realize they are just inexperienced and unclear on the difficulty.

I've been attacked, disrespected, rushed, misunderstood, under-valued for the good I have done and judged by friends and family because they didn't like my coping methods. Sometimes I feel the need to defend myself. Other times, I just let them think what they want. We are all just trying to make it out here.

I don't *need* people to understand my ongoing struggles, I just wish they wouldn't judge or minimize. It makes me angry to have my predicament brushed off like it's no big deal. I am fighting for my life every day. My challenges are big to ME and that *should* matter to a certain extent.

I've heard the phrases "let it go" or "get over it" more times than I care to remember but no one has ever told me how. I have a lot of residue; again, some parts of me are still that 5 or 6 year old girl.

While struggling, career has been my largest coping mechanism. In that arena, I'm passionate, meticulous, forward thinking, ambitious and have to be the best but, I don't always know when to slow down. I had something to prove and career made me feel empowered, worthy, capable, sharp and ahead of the game while I felt weak in my personal life.

After feeling burned out and stagnant working dead-end administrative jobs, I decided to use my degree and began a career in Criminal Justice. I applied to the Maryland Department of Public Safety and Correctional Services and became a Correctional Officer. This job led to an opportunity to instruct at a training academy which fulfilled my lifelong dream to teach. After three years, my role became a bit monotonous and I decided to step it up a notch. I applied to the Division of Parole and Probation, first becoming an Agent and progressively advanced into leadership. I hoped to help people and effect change.

Through that tenure, I had my share of struggles fitting in with some of my peers as well. They were okay with me when they felt I was at their level but any evidence of elevation caused a lot of tension and hate. It didn't stop them from utilizing me for my skills however, and I was still willing to help. I remained focused and continued to grow despite the snide remarks.

I was so focused on my career goals I once had a supervisor tell me, "Nova, you come to work in work mode and nothing else". I saw nothing wrong with that because it was something nobody could take away; I was going to be so on point they would never feel the need to. Constant achievement was a way to show I wasn't what I came from. I needed to allude to rising out of the ashes of my personal life like a phoenix. It was a great diversion.

As a person, I'm very type A. I've lived most of my life in disarray so I need structure and stability. I'm proactive, organized, responsible and hard on myself. I don't like to be blind-sided. The structure and stability I seek has helped me thrive but also keeps me up at night. I constantly worry about the future instead of focusing on the present.

Working for state government provided structure and job security and I did well but, as time progressed I started to feel frustration and burnout. I was also extremely dissatisfied with my leadership. The environment represented all that is wrong in the world without a definitive explanation of how to make it right. I mentored quite a few, am grateful for the lives I did impact and have seen a number of success stories however, functioning in that type of space became a downer. There was constant confusion in my life and career. *Resolve* is the key word here. Nothing in my career was finite and it paralleled the drama in my life; unresolved.

I tried to counteract the energy with holistic methods like acupuncture and meditation and even burned essential oils in a diffuser at home and in my office. I also attend motivational workshops quite often. They are all great methods but at that particular time, the stress would only subside for a bit. It always returned because I was dealing with things on the surface and not going deep enough to make an impact. I was busy trying to convince myself I was okay because I didn't want to face the dirty truth.

My heart was heavy and tears sat behind my eyelids on a daily basis, I was letting everything get to me. That was an indication that my pain and trauma were still fresh. I'm more cognizant and digging deeper now. I'm focused on forward movement, addressing the pain and coming to terms so I never feel the need to visit it again.

I'm diminishing self-doubt because I abhor the feeling I get in the pit of my stomach when I question if I love myself. I recently had someone ask me that exact question, "Do you love yourself?". I felt an uncomfortable feeling come over me, lowered my gaze and shrugged my shoulders. I responded, "I guess". He sat there for 20 minutes telling me how worthy I am while I sat there with a stoic look on my face. My youngest sister tells me all the time to stop criticizing myself. I always feel I can do better.

I also struggle with forgiveness, how to limit my interaction with toxic people and how to find balance between me and who I love. Growing up, I learned to adapt, not address. Today, for the first time, I'm optimistic, purposeful and diligent because I now know it's okay to be unapologetically happy, even if the people around me aren't.

Deep inside I know I'm beautiful, worthy, deserve happiness and bring great things to the table but, I'm working on exuding that so I begin to attract the same types of people. I have made a conscious decision to no longer be in the company of anyone who fails to see me in the same light because there's too much at stake at this point in my life. I've decided to be comfortable in my skin and continue to have compassion for people, even when it's not extended to me. It's okay to be me and allow people to be themselves.

CONCLUSION

Looking back on my choices and complacency in poor relationships, I realize I've been dealing more with people that have a need of me. I don't know many people willing to meet me in the middle. In fact, as an empath, I'm attracted to them for that exact reason, they "need" my help. They saw my vulnerability, inhibitions and pain and interpreted it as weakness. I allowed them to use my "hang-ups" to control me.

Some of my companions were gone for extended periods of time and I only saw them sporadically. I wasn't emotionally attached to them. It was the attachment through "title" and the occasional "validation" I loved. I loved the approval and compliments I got when they were pleased with me. The intimate requirements were limited. All I had to do was make sure they had the material things they required. I don't think they even gave a damn about love as long as I was meeting the need.

This cycle took a turn when I fell in love with my husband (He was only the second person I had ever been in love with). I was attached to him in every sense of the word and although he was away, I made every effort to see him as often as I could because, I wanted to be around him. I could switch my outlook on the relationship with the others when they showed me their true colors, even if I continued to deal with them. I couldn't do that with him.

It was so hard for me to emotionally detach even though he was hurting me. Truthfully, he reminded me the most of my father (his good qualities and some of his bad ones).

I deeply needed to feel loved and cared about and all the surface gestures satisfied that need for quite some time. I had a dwarfed perception of what love is and was supposed to feel like. These people were never meant to stay and subconsciously, I knew that. They served a purpose, as most people do in our lives. I connected with people who mirrored how I felt about myself because it was safe and comfortable. I never even thought about trying to date someone different (I got lucky with my child's father).

I've had an engagement ring stolen by my family and my clothing sold to strangers on the street by someone I loved very much and claimed to love me. I've been cheated on, lied to, held to a standard by people who couldn't even meet it, and physically and emotionally assaulted by people who said they loved me. How could I possibly identify, attract and accept real love? That's why it was so easy for me to throw it away after God blessed me with it.

I isolate because it's safe but it's also my way of taking time to be introspective. It's paramount to take a look at yourself first. I do my best thinking when I'm in my bedroom or car by myself. I've been completely unattached for 3 years and am just now learning not to feel lonely. My usual fix is to find a replacement. I refuse to do that now because I still have work to do. I'm not willing to throw away the progress I've made and quite frankly do not trust myself to choose wisely. I can't expect to attract someone who treats me well if I keep settling for those who don't. We teach people how to treat us.

If I work on myself and aim for my highest potential, God will bless me with a compatible being to share a healthy relationship with, I truly believe that. If he doesn't, my life won't fall apart because my cup will be full, it's a win-win situation. I want to be better; I have the ability to get better. Innately I've always known what was right for me but ego, trauma, outside influence, abandonment and immaturity caused me to deviate and refrain from listening to my spirit.

What people have put me through has not been about me per se; it was about where **THEY** were in their lives at the time. How I responded to it was about where **I** was in my life at the time. I could have exited stage left but I chose not to. I've beat myself up, felt hopeless and like I was digging myself out of a hole with a small spoon but by the grace of God, I've survived it all and maintained my sanity. I'm tapping into strength I didn't even know I had. That's clear evidence of my life's purpose.

Focusing on the positive keeps me in a much better headspace. I will good things into my life and when I fall short and deviate to the negative side, I put positive things in my ear to counteract it (i.e. meditation, Joyce Meyer and T.D. Jakes sermons). I even created a vision board with hopes of manifesting more positivity in my life. I know it's working.

I'm learning to own my part in my dysfunction and accept people for who they truly are, not who I want them to be. I realize people can only extend as far as their bandwidth will allow them. Forgiveness and discernment are the only way I'm ever going to be able to move forward successfully and in peace. People's mistreatment of me is not my burden to carry, my grandmother taught me that a long time ago. I guess that's why she could always be so light-hearted and forgiving.

There's weakness in being a victim and I'm far from weak. I felt sorry for myself because I wasn't being heard. Imagine looking for other people to fix your shit or tell you how to fix it. They're trying to figure out their own lives, they can't help me with mine. The people that steered clear of me because I wasn't vibrating high enough, I forgive them too.

I can't walk strong in my journey until I put my cares, fears and sorrow in the right person's hands...God. He'll take care of it, he always does. Even still, it has been so hard for me to surrender because I'm a control freak. I'm working on it and pray a lot. Prayer literally helped me start lifting my head off the pillow again. I began to feel hopeful when I started seeing the benefit of concentrating on what I could control. Submissiveness is not an easy feat but more often I submit and talk to God because I know he's listening.

I'm tapping into what really makes me happy and moving fearlessly. I even quit my good state job because I wasn't happy anymore and felt zero fear after I did it. I've since entered a new position but, those few months out of a traditional job gave me the break and jumpstart I needed and God sustained me; I never went without.

I felt relieved after I resigned because I wasn't being true to myself, a part of me was dying by the minute. I was adhering to the conventional way of thinking that you have to work for someone's huge entity to maintain stability. That's true to an extent but, you have to be happy and fulfilled and honestly, the owners of those huge entities were once someone with a big idea. The break got my creative juices flowing and made me look beyond conventionality. I'm getting out my own way and listening closer to my spirit because it never lies and now my best self is peeking from behind the shadows.

This book has been therapeutic for me. It has helped me release a stronghold and while people can certainly continue to hold my past against me, it won't affect me adversely anymore because I'm so much bigger than that.

"I told you so" will roll off my shoulders. Nobody can take my journey or growth away from me and that's where my power lies.

"Our lives are already written, the only thing we can change is our perspective"—DMX

Fear has held me back from reaching my fullest potential. It caused me to ruin a great relationship and some great opportunities. I add to my vision board constantly and am amazed at how many desires and goals I have for my life now that I'm focusing on myself more. I wake up every day eager to see new possibilities for my life. I'm feeling freer.

Guilt caused me to overcompensate with my son because I broke up our family. I also wanted to give him everything I didn't have and feared losing him as well. Although I raised him to be independent, fearless and strong, I never wanted him far from me. I was co-dependent on my own son. I sheltered him quite a bit and did everything I could to avoid him being hurt by anything or anyone.

I can't protect him from that. My job was to make constructive deposits in him, parent him and give him life skills and I did all of that. He has his own journey to travel and some of that is going to involve hurt and disappointment on both our parts. Believe me, he has hurt my feelings a few times because I felt rejected by him.

I know the resilience this young man has. I've spent my fair share of nights in hospitals watching him fight chronic asthma and battle pneumonia a few times from the age of two to eleven years old. In the interim, he played basketball and an instrument when people tried to deter him from it and he eventually conquered the asthma altogether. He's symptom free and has been for a number of years. I learn from him daily; the student schooling the teacher...HA! He's equipped. He will be fine and so will I.

Unconsciously, my world and a lot of my happiness was wrapped around him. No matter how tight I held on...Guess what? He grew up and moved on with life (as he should have). He told me he would be "out of my house by the age of 22 because he was a Man". He left at 21½, entered the military and has been stationed a large distance away over the past four years. He's thriving, meeting enormous goals and enjoying his independence.

Life and duty hinders him from coming home to visit often and he has started a family of his own. I'm still working on cutting the umbilical cord but he's forcing me to. It's not easy for a mother to disconnect from her child, especially when he's her only one. You carry this person under your heart for nine months, bond with and nurture them and in our case, grow up together. It was me and him against the world until he left the nest. HE was my friend and comfort when nothing else was going right in my life. HE was unconditional love.

We were so tight we could talk about any subject (deeply and transparent). He understood my temperament and provided balance because he's so level headed and I'm so much more high strung and emotional. We shared interests like hip hop music and sneakers, shared a room until he was ten years old and faced every adversity <u>together</u> since his birth. I could trust and count on him and he has always had the same in me.

When he chose to enter the military I went from seeing him every day to approximately every six months. I was proud of his courage and independent decision making because his back was never against the wall, he entered the military of his own volition. I cheered him on and supported every endeavor, but was lost without him in my immediate fold. In the beginning, I even slept in his bed sometimes.

Eventually, he met someone, told me she was the one, developed a serious relationship, became a father and got married. I found this young lady to be kind and loving toward my son and trusted his judgment; I connected with her immediately. I've always been very clear on the roles of mother and wife and have always told him when he got married and had a child, that unit should come first and would become his immediate family.

What I didn't mentally prepare for was the prospect of

157

feeling completely pushed to the side and void of a role in his life at all. I took for granted that our bond would sustain us.

Progressively, I'm learning every phase of our lives is navigation. When a person is inexperienced in a certain space, their navigation can become extreme and centralized until they find comfort juggling multiple things (one route at a time). During that time, something or someone is going to be slighted or neglected. We tend to concentrate on what's in our face.

(Me and my Soldier right after he completed Basic and Advanced Individual Training)

I've experienced that slight and neglect and although hurt, have had to force myself to be understanding, respectful, quiet, and supportive no matter what. It's hard but he's challenging me to trust the values I instilled in him. I know he'll figure out how to create balance at the end of the day. I miss him every day but am learning to appreciate that he lives his life on his own terms. Honestly, I admire him and see a lot of the healthy ME in him. He's quite the man and quite the go-getter. We all need time to come into our own; I'm still coming into my own as well.

Through trial and error, I learned some positive things about myself as well. I'm strong and don't give up easily. I'm a fighter. It takes a lot to knock me down and I always get back up. I'm very resourceful, not crazy about change but not inhibited by struggle or environmental issues. I adapt well and hit the ground running to improve any situation I'm faced with. I'm a risk taker, an explorer and a free spirit.

I'm driven, kind, humble, a good friend, and a survivor. I don't procrastinate. I'm a hustler and not apt to ask anyone for a hand-out. If I need money I make a way (legally). I've worked multiple jobs, all while attending graduate school full-time in order to better myself and create stability for us.

I continuously develop myself and have also worked unorthodox jobs, even if I was over-qualified. I've been a tour guide, waitress, cashier, cab dispatcher and for the past four years have been driving for Uber and Lyft as a part-time gig to supplement my full-time income. I stand by the logic that you can do anything you put your mind to as long as you put forth the effort; even if you're exhausted.

I'm a doer, not a talker and I don't believe in the word can't. My father has always told me, "throw the brick, you'll never know if you don't try". I follow that advice, do my best and take responsibility when I fall short. I pay forward, share knowledge, uplift others and through all of those great attributes, am still learning to be 100% comfortable in my skin. I'm more a giver than a taker and it's hard for me to tell people what I need. I used to be ashamed of some of my own unique qualities. I felt it was more important to fit in and sometimes, who I was didn't match up with who I was trying to be. I suffered for years putting up that facade. Those beauty marks make me special and I love being different; even down to my name (I hated it when I was younger).

Nova-*is a transient astronomical event that causes the sudden appearance of a bright, apparently "new" star and slowly returns to its original state over a few months.*

Latin meaning: New
Native American meaning: Chases butterfly

I'm trying different things and continue to be an over-achiever while also learning I don't have to reinvent the wheel. What I need is already inside me, I just have to tap into it. I've learned no accolade or amount of money will matter until I find my purpose. I'm good with who I really am even if it doesn't meet the status quo. Material things are just a perk, self-actualization and self-realization are the real gifts. I've had a myriad of accomplishments and was still broken inside because I was stuck in the past.

I couldn't even enjoy the fruits of my labor because I didn't feel worthy and believed I couldn't move forward without resolution of my past. Ego had me thinking people owed me an apology and I waited on it for years. An apology is a conscious decision, not an obligation. It represents accountability and some people are just not there yet.

I thought I needed atonement from my parents because I blamed them for my pain. I thought I needed outside sources to help me heal. My parents' apologies and willingness to take responsibility did give me relief, but it didn't get the job done. They initiated my pain but I allowed it to continue. They did their best and I still turned out well despite (that's how you show them better than you can tell them).

For years, *I was my own worst enemy.* I gave other people control of my destiny because I thought something was wrong with me and didn't find myself suitable to run my own life. No other flawed human should ever be given that power. I'm learning to be kind to myself and okay with being void of closure because there are many areas still left open. Honestly, I got closure when God decided to remove the adverse factors. He said, "It's Done".

I've literally had to withdraw and seclude to achieve this mindset and it's still an on-going process. I still beat myself up sometimes but am entitled to take the time I need to hurt and process. I had to remove the noise so I could hear my inner voice and have been called cold, mean and bitter because I did what I had to do to preserve my sanity and refused to tell people my business.

Point is, my life is no longer dependent upon anyone else's contribution, in any aspect. God knew we were going to fall short from the moment he created us. He gave us the gift of free will and that guarantees we will mess up sometimes. Often, we're out here running reckless until we gain the good sense to be obedient. If I wait on reciprocity or validation from others, life will continue to pass me by very quickly and I'll miss out on miraculous things. I don't want to miss out on anything else, I've lost enough.

LIFE is an independent journey and what YOU make it. Have you ever heard the saying "You come here alone and leave alone"? It's so true. It's ludicrous to sit and wait for someone else to light a fire under you. We should give ourselves the gift of receiving exactly what the universe has for us without compromise or outside opinion. We should also be mindful of what we exude because we attract what we give.

Thank you so much for purchasing my book and taking the time to read it. —*Nova*

PHOTO JOURNAL

Welcome to my photo journal!

The following pages represent my life depicted through Asana (Yoga Posture).

The beautiful thing about yoga is, it doesn't expect you to be perfect. Just do your best and it accepts you as you are. Through practice, you accomplish peace and awareness and develop confidence and mobility. The use of props (mat, blocks, straps, bolsters, blankets) aids in practicing with greater efficiency, ease and stability without hyper-extending.

Defined, Yoga is a spiritual and physical practice consisting of 8 stages. It uses breathing techniques, exercise and meditation to promote health and happiness and the ability to attain higher consciousness (*Merriam-Webster Dictionary/ quora.com*). Asana is one of the stages in Yoga.

Concept: Nova Walton-Marriott and Ashley Charles

Instructor: Martha McAlpine

Photographer: Lisa Fleet

Make-up: Nova Walton-Marriott

Hair: Anabel (Julia Dominican Salon)

Nova Walton-Marriott

Childhood Playfulness/Innocence

Sasangasana(Rabbit)

Significance: Deep physical and psychological memory of our time as infants

166

Abandonment/Trauma/Abuse/Challenges

Garudasana(Eagle)

Significance: Sustain, Preserve and Protect

Nova Walton-Marriott

True Love

Utthita Tadasana
(Standing Star)

Significance: Joy

Change/ Birth of my Son/ College

Vriksasana(Tree)

Significance: Balance and Empowerment

Grief/Heartbreak

169

Nova Walton-Marriott

Anjaneyasana
(Low Lunge)

Significance: Reaching toward the sky; wisdom sign or knowledge gesture

Vulnerability/Voids

Ustrasana(Camel)

Significance: Operating from a place of love, loving yourself

Anger/Ignorance/Ego

Nova Walton-Marriott

Virabhadrasana
(Warrior 2)

Significance: Natural response to emotions and mistakes.
We become warriors when we understand how to fight
our battles with proper weapons

Isolation/Surrender

Savasana(Corpse)

Significance: Relaxation and Recovery

Nova Walton-Marriott

Enlightenment

Bhujangasana(Cobra)

Significance: Rebirth and Self-realization

Renewal/Rising Above

Parighasana (Gate)

Significance: Closing the door on the past

Nova Walton-Marriott

Self-Awareness

Matsyasana(Fish)

Significance: Awareness and Opening the Heart

Illness/POWER

Significance: Look past the extra weight to the SCAR.

My stomach erupted from the inside out and I survived!

177

Nova Walton-Marriott

Gratitude

Anjali Mudra(Prayer)

Significance: To salutate and seal

Honoring and celebrating this moment

178

Additional photos from the session...

Gate Pose

Child's Pose

Gate Pose

AFTERWORD

I have known and had the pleasure of working with Nova over the past 4 years. I remember the woman who came through my doors, laying the broken pieces of her heart around her and wanting it to be whole again. I would get hour long glimpses into her life as it were now and learning about parts of her past that led to her present.

Upon reading the completed work I better understand Nova as a woman, a mother, a friend, and daughter. The trauma experienced from childhood into adulthood was not a hindrance but in many ways served as lessons in breaking old patterns.

There were many tears but also laughs on her journey and there will be many more of both in the coming years. Her story is one of resilience and determination to find her way through to the other side; not only more capable but stronger. And most importantly, to never stop growing.

-Hyeon-Jin Kwon